D1327393

THE DIVINE VISION

THE DIVINE VISION

Studies in the Poetry and Art of William Blake

born November 28th, 1757

by

KATHLEEN RAINE
VIVIAN DE SOLA PINTO
S. FOSTER DAMON
NORTHROP FRYE
KARL KIRALIS
PILOO NANAVUTTY
H. M. MARGOLIOUTH
MARTIN K. NURMI

and with an introductory poem by

WALTER DE LA MARE

Collected and Edited by

VIVIAN DE SOLA PINTO

for the William Blake Bicentenary Committee

HASKELL HOUSE PUBLISHERS LTD.
Publishers of Scarce Scholarly Books
NEW YORK, N. Y. 10012
1968

First Published 1957

HASKELL HOUSE PUBLISHERS LTD.
Publishers of Scarce Scholarly Books
280 LAFAYETTE STREET
NEW YORK, N. Y. 10012

Library of Congress Catalog Card Number: 68-24905

Haskell House Catalogue Item # 790

Printed in the United States of America

'Because he kept the Divine Vision in time of trouble'
Jerusalem, IV, 95, l. 20.

This book is dedicated to the memory of one of its chief begetters, Frank Heming Vaughan, the Secretary of the William Blake Bicentenary Committee, who died on 10th February, 1957. He was one of the 'builders in hope' who laboured nobly for the Divine Vision,

tho' Jerusalem wanders far away
Without the gates of Los, among the dark Satanic wheels.

Foreword

THE BICENTENARY OF the birth of William Blake is being celebrated by exhibitions and lectures in various parts of the English-speaking world and by the erection of a memorial in Westminster Abbey designed by Sir Jacob Epstein. To these tributes it has been thought fit to add the publication of a volume of essays and studies dealing with various aspects of Blake's work as a poet and artist by scholars from three continents.

The editor is particularly glad to be able to print at the head of the volume a short poem by the late Walter de la Mare, O.M., which was specially written for this purpose by Mr. de la Mare a few weeks before his death, and is probably the last poem that he wrote. Walter de la Mare is now with William Blake in eternity and it is fitting that his last poetic utterance was a salute to the poet to whose spiritual lineage he surely belonged.

The essays are arranged so as to fall into three main sections. The first two deal with Blake's early lyrics. The essay by Professor Foster Damon, the great American pioneer of modern Blake scholarship, on 'Blake and Milton' forms an appropriate transition to the theme of the major epics, *Milton* and *Jerusalem*. A fitting *coda* to this section is the essay by Piloo Nanavutty (Mrs. P. A. Jungalwalla), the distinguished Indian scholar, on 'William Blake and Hindu Creation Myths'. The last three essays are concerned with Blake as a pictorial artist.

An attempt has been made to select as some of the illustrations to this book pictures of Blake which have not been easily accessible. The great tempera painting discovered at Arlington Court in 1949 entitled 'The Cycle of Life' or 'The Sea of Time and Space' has, it is believed, been used here as a book-illustration for the first time, the beautiful water colour, 'She shall be called Woman', in the Metropolitan Museum, New York, is little known on this side of the Atlantic and the four designs which have been selected by Mr. H. M. Margoliouth to illustrate his article on 'Blake's Drawings for Young's *Night Thoughts*' have never before been reproduced.

The editor wishes, on behalf of the William Blake Bicentenary Committee, at whose request this work was undertaken, to thank the scholars who have contributed their essays to the collection without payment as contributions to the William Blake Bicentenary Fund, to which all the royalties earned by the volume are to be devoted. The main purpose of the fund is to defray the cost of the memorial to be erected in Westminster Abbey.

Acknowledgment is made to the Clarendon Press and *The Review of English Studies* for permission to reprint (in altered forms) the essays by H. M. Margoliouth and V. de S. Pinto, and to *A Journal of English Literary History* for permission to reprint the essay of Karl Kiralis.

V. DE S. PINTO.

University of Nottingham,
January, 1957.

Contents

List of Illustrations

A LIFETIME:
EPITAPH FOR WILLIAM BLAKE

I lived; I toiled—day in, day out,
Endless labour, shafts of bliss,
For three score years and ten,
    And then;
I watched, with speechless joy and grief,
My last and loveliest spring
    Take wing.

Think you, I grudged the travailing?—
I, who am come to this!

Walter de la Mare

I

The Little Girl Lost and Found and The Lapsed Soul

by

Kathleen Raine
Girton College, Cambridge (*Great Britain*)

I

The Little Girl Lost and Found and The Lapsed Soul

(i) *The Little Girl Lost and Found*

IN 1821 BLAKE PAINTED the beautiful tempera discovered at Arlington Court in 1949, and known as *The Cycle of the Life of Man*, or *The Sea of Time and Space.*[1] Professor Damon had, I believe, already surmised that this painting is neoplatonic in content; it is, in fact, a pictorial statement of the metaphysical theme developed by Porphyry in his *Cave of the Nymphs*, with certain details added from Blake's own study of the *Odyssey*. Not one symbolic figure or theme is of Blake's own invention, and a close study of the painting reveals Blake's profound understanding, and detailed knowledge, of the neoplatonic text. He was, in 1821, returning to a myth that had formed his thought some thirty years earlier; indeed so many of Blake's most characteristic symbols—the cave, the loom, the urns, the sea, the Four Worlds—are to be found here, that many Blake scholars have thought that this painting, far from being an illustration of a traditional myth, must be a very personal statement of Blake's own system. But Blake's myth was not an invention, in the modern sense of the word. All its elements are traditional, though the final result may be new in appearance. The truth is rather the reverse; Blake knew Porphyry very early in his poetic life, and adopted his symbolic terms from the outset. Porphyry's treatise was first published in English in 1788 in the second volume of Thomas Taylor's translation of Proclus' *Mathematical Commentaries*. It forms part

[1] Reproduced as the frontispiece to this volume.

of an essay *On the Restoration of the Platonic Theology by the Later Platonists.*[1] Blake evidently read Taylor's *Porphyry* on its first appearance, for the first unmistakable allusions to its symbolism appear in *The Book of Thel* (1789).[2]

Within the next four years Blake wrote three versions of Porphyry's theme of the descent of the soul into generation; and in more general terms, the theme persists in all his subsequent prophetic writings. First, *Thel* describes the soul who only looks down into the Cave of generation, and withdraws in horror, refusing to make the descent into this dark world; next, the two Lyca poems that carry the symbolic theme a little deeper; Lyca 'descends' into the cave of mortality; but she is safe among the wild beasts of the 'cavern' or 'den' of this world, and her awakening and return to eternity is foretold in the eight lines that preface the two poems, *The Little Girl Lost*, and *The Little Girl Found.* In 1793 came *Visions of the Daughters of Albion*, with Oothoon as the ravished Persephone, seized by a thunder-god of Hades as she gathers a golden flower. Oothoon willingly ventures herself where Thel feared to tread, into the world of the mysteries of sex and generation; she does not, like Lyca, fall into the sleep of oblivion; but she suffers, in the sea-girt cave of this world, from the conditions of the fallen world and its morality, so unlike that of the soul itself in eternity, as Oothoon continues, in her suffering, to proclaim.

[1] Taylor's translation of *The Cave of the Nymphs* was republished as a separate work in 1823.

[2] *Thel* is based upon Porphyry's theme of the descent of the feminine soul into generation; but general resemblance is no proof of direct influence. It is the minute particulars alone that reveal this. In the present instance, the mention in *Thel* of the Northern Gate through which souls enter the cave or grave of generation is decisive.

The Book of Thel reveals other influences besides that of Porphyry, but at the time of its writing the only neoplatonic texts that Blake is likely to have known are Porphyry, and Plotinus *Concerning the Beautiful.* When he came to write *The Little Girl Lost* and *Found,* he had also read with close attention another work, that is the immediate inspiration of the new poems, Thomas Taylor's *Dissertation upon the Mysteries of Eleusis and Dionysus.*[1] This excellent and intelligent exposition of a metaphysical theme deserves a place in the literature of the *philosophia perennis.* Whether or not Taylor correctly interprets the Mysteries as these were understood by those who instituted them, there is no doubt that he interprets them correctly as they were understood by Plotinus and his followers. The theme of the Mysteries of Eleusis is in essence the same as that of the Cave of the Nymphs—the descent of the soul from eternity into the temporal world, and its return to its native country. But, whereas Porphyry regards incarnation as a pure evil, as Thel does, Taylor in his *Dissertation* goes deeper, and

[1] At first sight there appear to be difficulties in supporting this view. The date of publication of the *Dissertation* is assumed to be 1790. There is, however, no date on the title-page, and the imprint of Amsterdam which it bears may be fictitious, since there is no record of its publication in the Dutch lists. The date 1790 is not a certainty, so far as the evidence exists. On the other hand, the date on the title-page of *Songs of Innocence* (1789) is not a publication date, and there is no evidence that a completed copy of the *Songs* did in fact exist in that year. The dates on Blake's title-pages prove no more than that he was at work on a particular book at that time. It was quite in character for Blake to begin work, in the energetic enthusiasm of a new inspiration, with the title-page as he did (so Sir Geoffrey Keynes informs me) with *Milton.* Beginnings, for Blake, were better than endings. Even if we suppose that most of the *Songs* were written by 1789, when the title-page was made, we cannot be sure that they all were. There was no fixed order assigned to the poems, and the arrangement of the plates remained variable for many years.

reveals another aspect of the Descent and Return, by which it may be understood as a necessary part of the divine plan. Upon this aspect of the myth Blake reflects in the story of Lyca. For Lyca, unlike Thel, descends, and she is safe in 'the caverns of the grave'.

The two poems *The Little Girl Lost* and *The Little Girl Found* may very well have been among the last that Blake wrote before he set to work on *Experience*; and that for two reasons. The first is that he later transferred these two poems to *Experience* when both series were completed; the second, that the eight opening lines of *The Little Girl Lost* were expanded into the *Introduction* and *Earth's Answer* that stand at the beginning of the second series of poems, and in fact serve as the enigmatic key to the mystery of Experience. *The Little Girl Lost* and *Found* may very well have been written as late as 1790, in a transitional phase of thought. There remains a third possibility that Blake saw Taylor's *Dissertation* in proof before the date of publication. This is not improbable, if we consider the likelihood of Blake's having known Taylor well at just that time. I see no difficulty in allowing that the two poems in question might have been written at a date that would permit of Taylor's influence. A very small overlap would suffice. Dr. Bronowski was, I think, the first to point out that Blake's poems were almost always an immediate record of his day-to-day reading or response to events. The same impulse of excitement that at times was only strong enough to inspire him to the writing of marginal comments, at other times set him writing poems or aphorisms of his own. So I believe it was with Taylor's *Dissertation*: no sooner read than Blake decided to try his hand at his own version of a theme to which he returned again and again. He had already attempted the theme in *Thel*, *Visions of the Daughters of Albion*, and the Books of *Los* and *Urizen* all take up variations upon this myth. *The Four Zoas* announces as its subject Albion's 'fall into Division & his Resurrection to Unity'—a process entirely Platonic, not only in its assumption of pre-existence and return (common to the several traditional branches of the *philosophia perennis*), but in its identification of this descent and return with the cosmic relation of the One and the Many. Blake's mythology at all times assumes the pre-existence of souls, a doctrine that is certainly not Christian.[1] Blake was aware of the philosophical difficulty in the official Christian position. Crabb Robinson reports a conversation with him (this was in his later years) on this subject:

> I suggested on philosophical grounds the impossibility of supposing an immortal being created an *a parte post* without an *a parte ante*. His eye brightened at this, and he fully concurred with me. 'To be sure, it is impossible. We are all co-existent with God, members of the Divine body. We are all partakers of the Divine nature.'

Whatever elements of the Platonic philosophy Blake rejected, this he preserved. He reconciled his Platonism with the Mosaic account of the creation of man 'from the dust of the earth' with the help of Christian Cabbalism, Gnosticism, and other esoteric systems. On his engraving of the Laocoon group [2] he wrote: 'Adam is only the Natural Man & not the Soul or

[1] The last Christian theologian to profess this doctrine was Origen, whose teaching was posthumously condemned in the year 534 by Pope Virgilius at the instance of Justinian.

[2] 1820.

Imagination'; 'He repented him that he had made Adam (of the Female, the Adamah) & it grieved him at his heart. What can be Created Can be Destroy'd.' Adam, made from the dust, is both created and destroyed; he is subject to death and knows no resurrection; while 'the immortal man that cannot die'—the imagination—comes from eternity and thither returns. This is not Christian, but it is undoubtedly Platonic.

The story of Lyca, in the two poems *The Little Girl Lost* and *Found*, is, then, Blake's version of the myth celebrated in the Mysteries of Eleusis, the story of the descent of Persephone into Hades, and the search of the Mother for her lost child. Taylor (and Blake closely follows him) interprets this myth as it was understood by the later Platonists: the Virgin Persephone is the soul descending into generation. Taylor quotes Olympiodorus's commentary on the *Phaedo*, where it is said, that

> the soul descends corically, or after the manner of Proserpine, into generation, but is distributed into generation Dionysiacally; and she is bound in the body Promethiacally and Titannically; she frees herself from its bonds by exercising the strength of Hercules; but she is collected into one through the assistance of Apollo and the saviour Minerva, by philosophising in a manner truly cathartic.

Apuleius is also quoted as an authority for regarding the myth of Persephone as an account of the descent of the soul into incarnation. The rape of Proserpine, we know from Apuleius, was exhibited among the symbolic shows of the Mysteries; and it there represented (so Taylor affirms) the descent of the soul and 'its union with the dark tenement of the body'. Taylor's version of the classical myth [1] is as follows:

> Proserpine, the daughter of Ceres and Jupiter, as she was gathering tender flowers, in the new spring, was ravished from her delightful abodes by Pluto; and being carried from thence through thick woods, and over a length of sea, was brought by Pluto into a cavern, the residence of departed spirits, over whom she afterwards ruled with absolute sway. But Ceres, upon discovering the loss of her daughter, with lighted torches, and girt with a serpent, wandered over the whole earth for the purpose of finding her till she came to Eleusina. There she found her daughter, and discovered to the Eleusinians the plantation of corn.

Taylor says that Ceres represents 'the self-inspective part of our nature, which we properly denominate intellect', and Proserpine 'the vital, self-moving and animating part which we call Soul',[2] Pluto 'signifies the whole of material nature', and the cavern, 'the entrance, as it were, into the profundities of such a nature, which is accomplished by the soul's union with this terrestrial body'. This seems to have been the passage that suggested to Blake the two poems that we are to consider. Lyca's story is that of Persephone.

[1] Taken from Minutius Felix.

[2] Intellect is here, it must be understood, used in the Platonic sense as that pure reason that is at once knowledge and the object of knowledge, and is above rational, or conceptual thought. In terms of Jungian psychology, Ceres would here be the Self, Proserpine the ego budded off, as daughter from mother. Only the ego descends into generation, the Self is not subject to temporal events. Whether or not Taylor gives a historically correct interpretation of the Eleusinian mysteries, it is a significant piece of symbolism in its own right.

The two stanzas that preface the first poem foretell the return of *the lapsed soul* [1] to her native country. These lines seem to be an early version of the longer and fuller *Introduction* and *Earth's Answer*, and will best be considered with them.

> In futurity
> I prophetic see
> That the earth from sleep
> (Grave the sentence deep)
>
> Shall arise and seek
> For her maker meek;
> And the desart wild
> Become a garden mild.

The sleeper, in *The Little Girl Lost* and *Found*, is Lyca; yet it is *earth* who will awake. This in some sense identifies Lyca as the Earth of *Earth's Answer*. Persephone was a goddess of vegetation whose return from Hades heralds the spring; and Blake has beautifully combined a classical and a Biblical myth in the flowering of the desert that is to follow the awakening of Earth. The passage from Isaiah that foretells that *the desert rejoice and blossom as the rose* is one to which Blake often returned. The conditions of its new blossoming are more fully described in *A Marriage of Heaven and Hell*. Suffice it here to point out the relation of the *Lyca* poems to the return of 'the dominion of Edom' prophesied in the *Marriage*.

What follows is based exactly on the Greek myth. Lyca [2] is

[1] The phrase *the lapsed soul* Blake appears to have derived from Plotinus, *On the Nature and Origin of Soul*, tr. Taylor. See below, p. 52.

[2] What is the origin of the name Lyca? The Greek root* λύκη (light) or λευκος (light, bright, white) is the most probable source. The soul as the

in some sense the individual soul descending into generation, and also, at the same time, the soul of the world. Her story is of a wandering and a return, a sleep and an awakening; for such, Plotinus taught, and Blake believed, is the story of

---

light of the body is a symbol not confined to Platonism; and the Earth in *Earth's Answer* is admonished 'fallen, fallen *light* renew'.

There is a minor character in the *Aeneid* named Lycus; there seems little connection between this Latian youth and Lyca, unless that he was

> . . . not like others born
> But from his wretched mother rip'd and torn.

Lyca might also be said to have been 'rip'd and torn' from her mother (although in another sense) in the process of her descent into generation. A more probable guess is perhaps another Lycus, whose name briefly appears in the Fourth Georgic, but in a landscape reminiscent not only of this poem of descent into caves, but of the cavernous descent shown to the virgin *Thel*. A mortal is permitted to visit the 'deep abodes' of the river goddess Arethusa. He travels downwards into his mother's *watery palace*, situated in *hollow caverns* under the *coral woods* of the sea's floor—a piece of symbolic landscape that Blake, given the key to the symbols by Taylor, could not have failed to read as signifying a descent into a material existence:

> He hears the crackling sound of coral woods,
> And sees the secret source of subterraneous floods
> And where, distinguished in their sev'ral cells,
> The fount of Phasis, and of Lycus dwells;
> Where swift Enipeus in his bed appears,
> And Tiber his majestic forehead rears.
>
> (Dryden's translation.)

Porphyry in his *Cave of the Nymphs* expounds the symbolism of rivers flowing from caverns as signifying the secret and mysterious sources of generation, within the world (which the cavern signifies). Lyca descends to be queen of subterranean abodes in the lion-king's 'palace deep', and herself becomes a source of generation, if we may conclude that the babes playing about her prostrate form, and that of the lion-king, in the accompanying design, are Lyca's children. But this may be fanciful speculation—for the obvious root is **λευκὸς**, the brightness doubly appropriate to an immortal and a virgin soul.

man's incarnation. The first of the two poems follows the action of the Lesser Mysteries of Eleusis that celebrated the rape of the maiden Persephone by the god of the underworld. Lyca's native home was

> In the southern clime
> Where the summer's prime
> Never fades away

This 'southern clime' one may read as the vales of Sicily, the flowery island where the daughter of Demeter dwelled before her rape; or, to read the eternal through the temporal, the intelligible world of light, where death and mutability have no place. Porphyry expounds at length a symbolism of North and South relating the southern and northern solstices to the two gates of Homer's Cave of the Nymphs. Blake had already in *The Book of Thel* adopted Porphyry's 'Northern Gate'; this strengthens the probability that he is using the symbol of the south also, in Porphyry's sense. In the South, souls enter immortality, in the North, generation. The South is, therefore, the abode of the gods and immortals; at the Northern gate, souls enter this world—as Lyca will presently do.

Lyca is, in an unexplained way, overcome with drowsiness. She lies down under the branches of a tree, and she summons sleep:

> Sweet sleep, come to me
> Underneath this tree.

The apparent naivety of the lines could not be more misleading: they are fraught with condensed traditional symbolic meaning.

The symbol of the Tree in Blake signifies always the natural universe, the vegetated condition of generation. One of the plates of *The Gates of Paradise* shows a woman pulling up a mandrake-child from the ground, under a weeping willow tree, another child, already gathered, in the folds of her dress. The accompanying text reads *I found him beneath a tree.* The tree of life is the tree of generation in a very literal sense. The *Genesis* myth has often been so interpreted. But Blake was thinking not only of *Genesis.* Trees and woods in classical mythology, Taylor argues,[1] are symbols of material nature; 'the word *silva,* as is well known, being used by ancient writers to signify matter'—from which we are to understand why Virgil makes Aeneas descend into the underworld *through a wood.* Here he quotes the passage from Book VI of the *Aeneid* that describes the hero's descent into the infernal regions; and here, I believe, is the original of the tree under which Lyca summons sleep. For at the entrance of Hades, there stands an elm, beneath whose branches reposes the god of sleep himself:

> In medio ramos annosaque brachia pandit
> Ulmus opaca ingens quam sedem somnia vulgo
> Vana tenere ferunt, foliisque sub omnibus haerent

—or, in Dryden's translation, (to which Blake would most likely have turned for an English version):

> Full in the midst of his infernal Road,
> An Elm displays her dusky Arms abroad:
> The God of Sleep here hides his heavy Head,
> And empty Dreams on ev'ry Leaf are spread.[2]

[1] *Dissertation.*

[2] Compare also 'Once a dream did weave a Shade
O'er my angel-guarded head.'

It is therefore entirely appropriate that Lyca should invoke sleep under the branches of a tree.

It is by no means easy to identify the trees depicted in the accompanying designs. In the first illustration, in which Lyca is seen half reclining under a tree, the black-and-white patches on the bark suggest rather the birch (the Celtic tree of death, as Blake would know from Percy's ballads) than the elm. Death and sleep are, in the symbolic language of neoplatonism, as for Blake himself, virtually synonymous. But that the tree shown in the third plate is an elm I would venture my botanical observation—and refer the reader to the plate in question. Only the great trunk is shown—*ingens*, as Virgil says—divided into two great boles that enwrap one another as they ascend. This habit is more common with the beech than with the elm; but I have seen elms that have grown in this way. In any case the detail is symbolic, not naturalistic, indicating the duality of the Tree of the Knowledge of Good and Evil. But Blake has been at pains to show the bark as heavily grained; and, while no leafy boughs are shown, there are many slender twigs emerging from the trunk itself—a well-known characteristic of the elm, and in particular of those pollarded hedgerow elms until recently such beautiful features of the landscape of the country round London. Blake must have seen such elms in abundance in his long country rambles into Kent and Middlesex.[1] This particular feature appears in no other tree illustrated in the *Songs*. There are willows, vines, a very presentable oak, dark forests of mere black trunks; but no other tree that could conceivably be an elm.

Lyca, then, longs to sleep; and appropriately summons the

[1] Browning observed 'the brushwood sheaf on the elm-tree bole' in his *Home Thoughts from Abroad*.

god of sleep and dreams under his own tree, the elm; but she fears that her mother will not wish her to sleep. This seemingly inexplicable and unmotherly prohibition can only be explained by reference to Taylor's definition of Demeter as the intellect, 'the self-inspective part of our nature', consciousness itself. Such a 'mother' will never willingly consent to the vegetating soul's lapse into the sleep or death, the Lethean forgetfulness, that is consequent upon a descent into generation. The descending soul, sinking into the *amnesis* that for the Platonists was the essential characteristic of the generated soul, must somehow escape the vigilance of the intelligible word, here symbolized as the mother:

> How can Lyca sleep
> If her mother weep,

but the descending soul itself wishes only to generate; Porphyry at length describes the intense desire of the 'moist' souls to descend, as Lyca wishes to descend, into generation:

> If my mother sleep
> Lyca shall not weep.

If the story were simply that of a lost little girl being sought by her parents, this would be nonsensical: no mother would refuse sleep to her weary child; and no child lost in a forest would give as a reason for her inability to sleep, her mother's vigilance. Fear might keep her awake, or the anxiety at *not* being found by her parents, but not, conceivably, the opposite fear here described—that *of being found*. Nor, conceivably, would the daughter dry her tears at the thought that her mother has given up the search for her, and fallen asleep. But Blake's story is myth pure and simple. The mother is the higher consciousness that opposes the lapse of the soul into its temporal dream. In these terms, Lyca's statement that she cannot sleep while her mother is vigilant, but will gladly do so when that vigilance is withdrawn, is very easily understood. Lyca has come to the place of the People of Dreams, who gather about the galaxy of the fixed stars, and will presently follow her desire to descend into the dream-world of bodily existence to which her drowsiness so strongly attracts her; 'For to be plunged in matter, is to descend into Hades, and there fall asleep.' Earthly existence as a *dream* is one of Blake's favourite symbols—the dream of the lost Emmet, 'the lost Traveller's dream under the hill', 'The deadly dreams that the soul falls into when it leaves Paradise following the serpent'; and so with the symbol of sleep, or 'deadly sleep' that is used so powerfully to describe the condition of fallen Albion; and it is by the Platonic *anamnesis*—a reversal of the Lethean forgetting that is the condition of birth in this world—that Blake sees man's return to Paradise. To awaken man from his sleep is Blake's constant purpose.

Blake would have been familiar, from Taylor's Porphyry, with the view that it is 'pleasure which draws souls downward to generation'. The Goddess Night advises Jupiter to make use of honey [1] as an artifice to ensnare the god Saturn:

[1] Compare Yeats: What youthful mother, a shape upon her lap
Honey of generation has betrayed,
And that must sleep, shriek, struggle to escape
As recollection or the drug decide.
(*Among Schoolchildren.*)

Recollection is *anamnesis*, the drug the Lethean drink.

> When stretch'd beneath the lofty oaks you view
> Saturn, with honey by the bees produc'd,
> Sunk in ebriety, fast bind the God.

> . . . the theologists obscurely signifying by this, that divine natures become through pleasure bound, and drawn down into the realms of generation.

This pleasure, symbolized as honey, is 'the pleasure arising from copulation'. In the same work, Blake would have found quoted the passages from the *Phaedo* describing the souls drinking the waters of forgetfulness, 'the new drink of matter's impetuous flood, through which the soul, becoming defiled and heavy, is drawn into a terrene situation'. Clearly Lyca's desire for sleep is of this order—the irresistible desire of sexual pleasure through which the soul comes to drink the honeyed cup of generation. Blake describes Lyca as *seven summers old*; but in the first design she is shown as a nubile virgin, and in the last, as (presumably) the mother of the babes playing round her. The number seven is symbolic in quite another sense.

Plotinus gives similar reasons. The descent is at once a sin and a punishment for sin, a fate at once irresistible and voluntary, like Lyca's drowsiness, 'since necessity has that which is voluntary united with its nature'.[1]

Lyca, then, like Persephone, falls into this danger through a temporary separation from her mother. Ceres left her daughter unguarded in Sicily, and Persephone wandered out into the meadows, gathering flowers. Lyca, apparently without fear and following, like Persephone in Ida, only her own pleasure had

> . . . wander'd long
> Hearing sweet birds' song.

[1] *On the Descent of the Soul.*

In the Greek myth, the rape is unsought by Persephone [1]; but in Blake's telling of the myth, it is the soul herself who wishes to descend. This is perfectly comprehensible if we consider the length at which Porphyry dwells upon the soul's *desire* to generate.

Lyca, at the foot of the tree of sleep, summons the powers of darkness, night, and the moon, who are all traditionally associated with the entry of souls into generation:

> Frowning, frowning night,
> O'er this desart bright
> Let thy moon arise
> While I close my eyes.

Plato tells that the souls descend into incarnation at midnight, 'this period being peculiarly accommodated to the darkness and oblivion of a corporeal nature; and to this circumstance the nocturnal celebration of the mysteries doubtless alluded' [2]—so Taylor comments. The moon, according to Proclus,[3] 'is the cause of nature to mortals', and her association with the descent of souls into birth and generation is described at length by Porphyry. He further tells us that the Tropic of Cancer is attributed to the Moon, because this tropic—the Northern Gate—is that through which souls descend to earth. This is explained by Porphyry as being so because (for men dwelling in the Northern hemisphere) Cancer is the tropic nearest to

[1] Who does, nevertheless, incur it by gathering the flower of the hundred-headed golden Narcissus. Blake's Oothoon is raped by Bromion after gathering a golden flower, the 'Mary gold'.

[2] *Dissertation.* The traditional midnight celebration of the Christmas Mass no doubt perpetuates this ancient belief about the time of incarnation.

[3] Commentary on the *Timaeus.* Quoted by Porphyry.

the earth. It is in the lunar house of Cancer that the souls drink

> the starry cup placed between Cancer and the Lion, a symbol of this mystic truth, signifying that descending souls first experience intoxication in that part of the heavens through the influx of matter. Hence oblivion, the companion of intoxication, there begins silently to creep into the recesses of the soul.[1]

There is no mention of the Northern Gate in the poems of *Lyca*; but another of Blake's incarnating virgins—Thel—comes to that gate, which she refuses to enter, though she looks down when

> The eternal gates' terrific porter lifted *the northern bar.*

Los, who controls generation, is the keeper of *the gates,* and of the North, where souls descend. It is in *The Cave of the Nymphs* that we have the source of Blake's northern gate symbolism, and it is to the same text that we must refer for other symbols relating to the Zodiac.

Blake makes no mention of the sign of Cancer. He does, however, introduce the next sign of the Zodiac—the Lion; for the Lion—as we ought to expect— makes his appearance just at that point in the narrative at which Lyca has sunk into oblivion in presumably the lunar house of Cancer. She has now passed the frontiers of generation, and entered the circles of the planets who control destiny and a new existence awaits her. In the myth of Persephone, it is Pluto who bears the virgin away

[1] Macrobius. Quoted in a footnote to Porphyry, *op. cit.*

to his subterranean palace; and why Blake chose to substitute a lion for Pluto will be made clear by a further quotation from Macrobius:

> Pythagoras thought that *the empirè of Pluto began downwards from the milky way,* because souls falling from thence appear to have already receded from the Gods. . . . On this account, since those who are about to descend are yet in *Cancer*, and have not left the milly way, they rank in the order of the Gods. *But when, by falling, they arrive at the Lion, in this constellation they enter on the exordium of their future condition:* And because, in the *Lion*, the rudiments of birth, and certain primary exercises on human nature commence; but *Aquarius* is opposite to the *Lion* . . . hence when the sun is in *Aauarius*, funeral rites are performed to departed souls.[1]

This is precisely the situation in which Lyca encounters the Lion; she is at the beginning of her human incarnation,—the 'exordium of her future condition'. She enters the empire of Pluto (that is, this world, where the souls are 'dead to eternity'), *when she arrives at the lion*, for here she is no longer in the world of the gods, but in that of generation. Lyca is, from this point on, throughout the remaining verses of the two poems, *asleep*. She has forgotten her former life, and is in the condition of those souls who in Plato's myth of Er have drunk the waters of Lethe. In her sleep, she is conveyed by the Lion and Lioness to 'caves'—the 'caverns deep' of Pluto's kingdom, Plato's and Porphyry's cave of the world.

Plato's strange myth in the *Phaedo* distinguishes between the true earth, and the apparent earth in which mankind dwells;

[1] Macrobius, quoted by Taylor in a note to Porphyry, *op. cit.* Italics mine.

this apparent earth consists of caves—misty hollows into which only a feeble glimmer of the true light reaches mankind. Blake had read Porphyry's philosophic exposition of this mythology long before he read Plato. Blake made extensive and masterly use of the cave symbol. It appears in the poem *Night*, in which the angels 'visit caves of every beast'. In the prophetic books, caves and dens, as places of material existence, and 'the caverned man' as the man shut away from eternity within a body, or a world, are recurring themes. The binding of Urizen describes the encaverning of the eternal mind within the skull. There can be little doubt that Blake's earliest knowledge of this cave symbol came from Porphyry's work:

> The ancients, indeed, very properly consecrated a cave to the world. . . . Hence they considered earth as a symbol of that matter of which the world consists; on which account some thought that matter and earth are the same, through the cave indicating the world, which was generated from matter.

The Cave of the Nymphs on the coast of Ithaca that Homer describes in the *Odyssey* is such a world-symbol; and it is sacred to the Naiads, nymphs of generation. This cave is dark, yet at the same time beautiful:

> Through matter, therefore, the world is obscure and dark; but through the connecting power, and orderly distribution of form from which also it is called *world*, it is beautiful and delightful. Hence it may very properly be denominated a cave: as very lovely, indeed, to him who first enters into it, through its participation of forms, but obscure to him who

surveys its foundation, and examines it with an intellectual eye. So that its exterior and superficial parts, indeed, are pleasant, but its interior and profound parts are obscure, and its very bottom is darkness itself.[1]

Porphyry goes on to describe the flowery caves of Mithra, and other 'rites pertaining to the mysteries of caverns and dens', which were, he says, dedicated to the world: 'From hence, as it appears to me, the Pythagoreans, and after them Plato, showed that the world is a cavern and a den.' Plato also calls his cave a prison.

The lion-king finds Lyca on 'hallow'd ground', and there seems no more likely explanation of this, than what Blake knew from Porphyry of the cave as a place sacred to the world-spirit, to Mithra, or to the Naiades. Caves were, Porphyry says, the earliest shrines, and, in Mithraism, places of initiation. It is into such a sacred place that the sleeping maid is carried by the Lion, in whose house she enters upon her 'future condition' (in the den of the world), which is at once that of a generated soul, and of marriage; for 'Souls proceeding into generation are the Nymphs called Naiads. Hence it is usual to call those that are married Nymphs, as being conjoined to generation'. The words of the Lion-king in *A Little Girl Found*, 'In my caverns deep Lyca lies asleep' state concisely the condition of the generated soul in the world-cave, in the symbolic language of the Platonists.

In this nocturnal underworld, animal forms play about the sleeping Lyca:

> Leopards, tygers, play
> Round her as she lay.

[1] Porphyry.

This requires little explanation; it is obvious that animal forms are native to the natural world. But it may be that Blake was here again thinking of Virgil's account of the descent into Hades, in whose cavernous entrance, once the elm-tree is passed, monstrous forms encounter the traveller:

Multaque praeterea variarum monstra ferarum

Animal existences are, in the Neoplatonic symbolism, creatures of the world of generation; for only souls belong to eternity.

Taylor's account of the Mysteries of Eleusis represents this mystery of generation as one of double aspect—from the point of view of the eternals, (represented by Demeter) a disaster, yet from the other side—that of Hades—the greatest blessing. Plotinus wrote that

> the descent of intellect into the realms of generation becomes, indeed, the greatest benefit and ornament which a material nature is capable of recovering; for without the participation of intellect in the lowest regions of matter, nothing but irrational soul and a brutal life would subsist in its dark and fluctuating abode.

Zeus, in the myth, overrules Demeter's protestations, and permits and enables the king of Hades to carry off the Maiden. Taylor quotes Claudian's poem on the Rape of Proserpine, in which the holy significance of this marriage is stressed. The account seems to foreshadow the myths associated with Jesus in the Harrowing of Hell and the freeing of the imprisoned souls. It is said that on the night of the marriage of Persephone all the souls in Hades rejoiced; that no souls descended into the underworld, and that Charon the ferryman rowed his empty boat on the river of Lethe, singing. The descent of Persephone, like that of Jesus, brings hope to the souls in darkness, which is illumined by the presence of a heavenly nature.

Blake follows this traditional understanding of the mystery, in describing the joy of the beasts at Lyca's presence. The Lion gambols and weeps for joy, and no harm is offered to the sleeping maiden. Plato also in the *Timaeus*

> both praises the world and calls it a blessed god, and asserts that the soul was given to the universe by its beneficent artificer, that it might possess an intellectual condition; hence it is requisite that the world should be intellectual, which cannot take place without the intervention of soul. Hence soul was infused into the universe on this account; and each of our souls was in a similar manner inserted into body, as necessary to the perfection of the whole. For it is requisite that as many and similar genera of animals should be contained in the sensible, as abide in the intelligible world.

This would seem to be the philosophy implicit in *The Little Girl Lost*.

The second of the two poems takes up the theme of the Greater Mysteries, in which were celebrated the Great Mother's search for her lost daughter. Demeter, inconsolable, sets out on her long wanderings in search of Persephone; and the wanderings of Lyca's parents is but a paraphrase of the myth:

> All the night in woe
> Lyca's parents go
> Over valleys deep,
> While the desarts weep.

Tired and woe-begone,
Hoarse with making moan,
Arm in arm seven days
They trac'd the desart ways.

The presence of two parents in Blake's poem might seem an obstacle to this view. But it is strikingly evident that only the mother counts. In the first of the poems the father is not even mentioned, and he plays only a passive role in the second. It is the mother's vigilance that prevents the virgin's falling asleep; and it is the mother's grief that is stressed in *The Little Girl Found*:

Rising from unrest
The trembling woman prest
With feet of weary woe
She could no farther go.

This is the very essence of the old story of the wandering Mother-goddess of Eleusis, who refused all rest and comfort as she travelled the earth seeking for her child. Moreover, Demeter did not travel alone; she was accompanied by Dionysus, whose presence Taylor describes, together with conjectured philosophical reasons why he should have been there.

Just as Persephone descends into night (who, personified, presides over the nuptial couch of Pluto and his bride [1]) so in her turn the Mother—intellect—must descend into the night of this world to seek for her lost daughter, the incarnating soul. Lyca, in the first of the two poems, invokes 'frowning, frowning, night'; and very properly, since (so Taylor comments on

[1] Claudian, *op. cit.*

Claudian) 'the soul through her union with a material body becomes familiar with darkness, and subject to the empire of night, in consequence of which she dwells wholly with delusive phantoms'—the shades of Hades. Claudian describes Persephone's 'appearing in a dream to Ceres, bewailing her captive and miserable condition, for such indeed is the wretched condition of the soul when profoundly merged in a corporeal nature'. Taylor (who himself followed Porphyry in his extreme rejection of the physical world and the body), is here stating the truth as it appears from the point of view of the intelligible world. From the point of view of the immortal mother, the daughter's descent is so understood; Lyca's parents also

> . . . dream they see their child
> Starv'd in desart wild.
>
> Pale, thro' pathless ways
> The fancied image strays
> Famish'd, weeping, weak,
> With hollow piteous shriek.

Taylor does not make any mention of Persephone's refusal of food in Hades; but Blake's *famish'd* suggests that he also knew other versions of the myth, which include the well-known episode of the eating of the seven seeds of a pomegranate. This Blake might well have added from Ovid's *Metamorphoses*, a book he knew well, and certainly before 1790.[1] Jupiter tells Ceres that she may bring back her child to Olympus only on the condition that she shall have eaten no food in Hades.

[1] Daphne changed into a laurel is illustrated on an early page of the Rossetti manuscript.

Persephone has eaten nothing in her captivity but seven seeds of a pomegranate; and for this it is ordained that she shall remain in Hades for one half of the year and return to the world of the celestial gods for the other.

Here we may have the source of the number seven that appears as a recurrent and inexplicable theme in the two Lyca poems. Lyca is 'seven summers old' at the time of her descent into the caverns; and her parents sought her for seven days and nights:

> Arm in arm seven days
> They trac'd the desert ways
>
> Seven nights they sleep
> Among shadows deep

—and on the eighth, they meet the Lion. The seven seeds might seem, from the Ovid version of the myth, to be a measure of time, since they determine the partition of Persephone's year, above and below. Can it be that Blake, also, has related the number seven to the progression of the Zodiac, from the beginning of the year? From Capricorn to the Lion is a space of seven months; were Lyca's seven 'years' her progress through the heavenly houses, until, between Cancer and Leo, she reached the Northern Gate through which she must descend? The long passage by Macrobius quoted by Taylor in a note on Porphyry contains a great deal of information about the incarnation of souls in relation to the Zodiac, and the suggestion is not far-fetched that Blake may have had this symbolism in mind. Lyca enters incarnation in the seventh sign; and the parents, also, sought for their daughter seven days, and on the eighth came in their turn to the sign of the Lion:

> Till before their way
> A couching lion lay.
>
> 'Follow me' he said;
> 'Weep not for the maid;
> In my palace deep
> Lyca lies asleep.'

The number seven also occurs in Plato's mythology. The souls returning to incarnation, having been allotted their lives, for *seven days* travel across a desert, hot and dry, and at the end of this journey, reach the waters of Lethe (matter), whose oblivion they drink and immediately 'descend' into generation.

The 'palace deep' of Hades is described by Virgil in the sixth book of the *Aeneid*; it is a *golden* palace; and the traditional association of gold with the underworld was, besides, known to Blake from Milton and elsewhere. He would have had in mind of Milton's Pandemonium :[1]

> . . . Soon had his crew
> Op'nd into the Hill a spacious wound
> And dig'd out ribs of Gold. Let none admire
> That riches grow in Hell; that soyle may best
> Deserve the pretious bane . . .

The gold of the underworld has, in Blake's poem, transferred itself to the Lion-king himself, who is

[1] *Paradise Lost*, Book I, 688–92.

A spirit arm'd in gold.

On his head a crown,
On his shoulders down
Flow'd his golden hair.
Gone was all their care.

The hidden gold of Hades Blake has interpreted as the spiritual 'gold' of the golden Age, the golden world of Eden—and perhaps in this he is rightly interpreting the classical myth. The King of Hades is not, after all, iron-clad in the dress of the fallen world; he is golden, divine. So according to some classical sources, the Zeus of the underworld is in truth the same as the Zeus of Olympus, and Persephone's marriage in truth a marriage to the supreme deity himself. This teaching is akin to the teaching of the alchemists, familiar to Blake, 'that which is beneath is like that which is above and that which is above is like that which is beneath'. It is this revelation to the parents that is the central meaning of the poem. Here, as in *Thel,* Blake is answering the neoplatonists with their mistrust of matter, with the philosophy of the Alchemists, of Agrippa and Paracelsus, whom he passionately admired, as he himself says.

In the 'palace deep' the parents find their child sleeping safe among 'tygers wild', and they themself remain in the Lions' kingdom

To this day they dwell
In a lonely dell
Nor fear the wolvish howl
Nor the lion's growl.

Lyca is still in her sleep to the end of the poem. Blake made no question but that the generated soul is sunk into unconsciousness, and the promised awakening is foreseen only in the remote future,

> When the earth from sleep
> Shall arise and seek
> For her maker meek.

Here one may stop to consider this early essay in mythological composition. Jung and Kerenyi see the essence of myth in the action and movement of symbolic personification; and in this sense I use the word of certain of Blake's poems. Other poems in the *Song of Innocence* tend to be symbolic rather than mythological; or at most, the spiritual beings (the child on the cloud, or the supernatural figures in *Night* or *A Dream*) perform only some one single action. But in the two Lyca poems we have supernatural figures (gods or spirits, certainly not human persons) not only characterized (like the child on the cloud) but also going through a complete symbolic drama, universal in its significance, and, in its final analysis, inexplicable in rational terms—a mystery in the religious sense of the word. Lyca is not a human child, like the Little Black Boy or the Chimney-sweepers; she is a universal aspect of humanity, archetypal. All the human and animal personifications in this poem clothe supernatural beings, archetypal forces. Myth is at once a metaphysical and an artistic creation—metaphysical in content, but aesthetic in the clothing of those divine forms and the symbolic landscape they inhabit. This handling of mythological themes is one of the proper elements of poetry, though seldom found in the writings of modern poets, and little valued where it is present by a generation to whom the imaginative world of which myth is the proper and only expression, is for the most part as if non-existent.

What it is above all important to realise is that Blake did not rely upon his own invention, but adapted traditional material. Maybe a blind plunge into the world of the archetypes will bring to the surface all that ancient wisdom has over centuries pieced together of knowledge of the gods; but I have yet to find that any major poet ever relied upon this kind of 'inspiration'. Blake did not do so. As a draughtsman, he was from his earliest youth accustomed to copying—from the Gothic tombs of Westminster Abbey, from drawings of Raphael and Michelangelo. His collection of prints, begun in his boyhood, is believed to have been both large and remarkable. He was a great reader. He had not the modern habit of mind that disdains tradition. He worked from models—and his originality lies not in his invention of new themes, but in the genius with which he made use of old—wherein, indeed, he was no different from any other significant poet. Imagination—Coleridge's *esemplastic power*—fuses and re-creates whatever is in the mind; it does not *invent*, in the vulgar modern sense. How completely the material has been transformed by Blake in these two poems is evident from the fact that it has not, so far as I know, hitherto been pointed out that Blake was working from the Greek myth. What is more, the poem fails at precisely those points at which the material has not been completely integrated within the poet's imagination—the rather didactic discussion of the conditions that will permit Lyca to sleep. Here the poem is obscure not because it is a formless product of personal fancy, but because traditional material has been introduced that has not been sufficiently transformed in the fires of imagination. It is, I believe, nearly always for this reason that Blake's poetry fails, and not, as has often been supposed, because of his too great reliance upon his visions.

All that Blake has essentially changed in the Lyca poems, as compared with the Greek myth, are the names. This is perfectly right, because names are accidental, belonging to a particular time, place, and civilization. The essences are immortal. Re-naming and re-clothing the gods is one of the tasks of the makers of culture. The old Greek names were outworn. New names eliminate merely historical associations and make a new and direct link between the myth and the eternal world that it reveals. This is precisely what Blake intended to do, and what he has done. But he could not have done so without profound reflection upon the earlier models of man's attempts to state the same unchanging theme.[1] This, it seems to me, is the

[1] There is already a psychological element in the Neoplatonic interpretations of the theme of the Soul's descent. Plotinus wrote that 'the whole soul does not enter the body, but something belonging to it always abides in the intelligible, and something different in the sensible world'. The relation of Persephone to Ceres is, on one level, psychological; and the relation between the unconscious sleeping generated part of the soul, to the all-knowing eternal part, may well have given Blake the first suggestion of themes that he later made his own—the relation between the spectral selfhood and the eternal humanity, the Imagination. The present time may find assistance in the understanding of this relationship with the aid of Jungian psychology. Jung's account of the relation between the Self (Blake's Humanity) and the ego (Blake's selfhood) is, also, that of a part (a complex) budded off from the whole—a mother-daughter relationship, one may say.

Thus understood, we may pause to admire the wisdom of the Neoplatonic myth (for to say that the old Mysteries of Eleusis really held this meaning is a different matter) by which the Mother seeks the Child; it is the eternal that seeks the temporal, the divine that seeks the human, as the vision seeks the visionary. A similar meaning may be found in the *Book of Revelation*, that describes Christ, 'behold I stand at the door and knock'. Blake later made

right way for a poet to use his material. His sources should not be evident in the finished work, but they should be very fully understood by the poet himself.

---

great use of this relationship between the Divine Humanity and the sleeper, temporal man. Imagination, Blake ever held, is the active principle, fallen man the passive. The myth of the mother who seeks her sleeping child is, in this case, a foreshadowing of the later theme that is central in *The Four Zoas* and in *Jerusalem*.

(ii) *The Lapsed Soul*

Blake's preoccupation with the theme of the soul's descent and return is already beginning to be apparent in *The Book of Thel* (1789). The two Lyca poems state the theme more fully, and show Blake's interest shifting from the world of eternity (Innocence) to that of generation (Experience), Lyca's caverns, Persephone's Hades. *Songs of Experience* all in one way or another are concerned with the nature of things in this underworld in which we are now living; with the soul's sufferings in that world, or with its longing to return to eternity, or with the cruel laws to which mankind is here subject. Blake's *Experience* is Plato's cave, Plotinus's Hades.

With good reason, then, Blake placed at the beginning of the series the two poems *Introduction* and *Earth's Answer.* All the poems that follow are given their context by these two grand and sombre poems. They are an expanded version of the opening lines of *The Little Girl Lost*:

> In futurity
> I prophetic see
> That the earth from sleep
> (Grave the answer deep)
>
> Shall arise and seek
> For her maker meek;
> And the desart wild
> Become a garden mild.

The title-page of *Songs of Experience* is dated 1794; in that year Taylor's *Five Books of Plotinus* appeared, and its impact is promptly reflected in Blake's poems of that time. The differences between the Lyca poems and *Introduction* and *Earth's Answer* can nearly all be traced to the added influence of Plotinus. Not only is this so in the details of imagery and implicit metaphysics, but also, I would venture to say, in a certain noble solemnity that has not hitherto been a note struck by Blake. It is the echo of the voice of Greek philosophy.

Plotinus's vocabulary, as Taylor translates it, is more easily traced. From this time appear such terms as the *descent* or *lapse* of the soul; the *sleep* or *death* of the incarnate soul immersed in the *grave* of matter; the world of *generation*; temporal being as the *shadow* of the eternal, and temporal man as *the shadowy man*.[1] The body is *mire* or *clay*, from which the face of the spirit must be *cleansed*; the *fluctuating* surface of nature; the *cave* or *den* or *prison* of the world are a few examples of this terminology.

The phrase *the lapsed soul* that occurs in the *Introduction* comes, appropriately enough, from Plotinus *On the Nature and Origin of Evil*. Plotinus argues that the soul's descent into a world of matter is the only source of evil. Her true country is the world of *divine light*. Falling into matter, she falls into *darkness*, and into *the watery element* (matter is symbolized by Plotinus as *water* or occasionally *mire*), and there she must wait in captivity for *the break of day* that will restore her to her native place:

> Matter obscures by sordid mixture the light which emanates from the soul; by opposing the waters of generation, she

[1] cf. Then Roll'd the shadowy man away
From the Limbs of Jesus. (*The Everlasting Gospel.*)

occasions the soul's entrance into the rapid stream, and by this means renders her light, itself vigorous and pure, polluted and feeble, like the faint glimmerings of a watch tower beheld in a storm. For if matter was never present, the soul would never approach to generation; *and this is the lapse of the soul, thus to descend into matter.*[1]

In Blake's poem 'the voice of the Bard' (*Songs of Experience*, 'Introduction')—imagination—reminds the soul of her native state:

> Calling the lapsed Soul
> And weeping in the evening dew;
> That might controll
> The starry pole,
> And fallen, fallen light renew.

The lapsed soul and the fallen light both, so it seems to me, are taken from the passage quoted. A further quotation from Plotinus throws light on *the slumbrous mass* in the third stanza:

> The vicious man therefore dies, so far as the soul can die, and the death of the soul is both while merged in body, to descend into matter and be filled with its darkness and deformity, and after it lays aside body, to return into it again, till after proper purification it rises to things superior, *and elevates its eye from the sordid mass*: for indeed, to descend into Hades and *fall asleep in its dreary regions*, means nothing more than to be profoundly merged in the filth and obscurity of body.[1]

[1] Italics mine.

Blake has simply condensed 'the sordid mass' and the concept of sleep that immediately follows into his fine phrase, *the slumbrous mass*:

> O Earth, O Earth, return.
> Arise from out the dewy grass;
> Night is worn
> And the morn
> Rises from the slumbrous mass.

The soul of the world has fallen asleep, held captive, like Persephone in Hades. The myth that was left incomplete in *The Little Girl Lost* and *Found* is taken up at the point of its incompletion: the time has now come for the re-ascent of the soul from Hades into the world of light. Earth, and the lapsed soul, are both in a sense Lyca, who is also at once the individual generating soul, and the soul of the world, whose mysteries were celebrated in the Eleusinian rites of the two Goddesses.

Earth is told that

> The starry floor
> The wat'ry shore
> Is given thee till the break of day.

Lyca was young: earth is old,

> And her locks cover'd with grey despair.

Lyca descended through the Northern Gate, Earth must re-ascend through the Southern. She is now waiting for the new dawn of eternity by the shores of the waters of matter, the sea of time and space. The stars, rulers of destiny, are, perhaps, the 'stars beneath' of the alchemists, the 'nether sky' of Blake's *Memorable Fancy.*[1] The landscape is appropriate to the soul in a prison of matter and darkness. *The wat'ry shore* is the material universe—

> . . . dire-resounding Hyle's mighty flood[2]

Blake must also have known Taylor's short essay *On the Wanderings of Ulysses,* published together with his Porphyry, whose essence is thus summarized:

> . . . the person of Ulysses, in the Odyssey, represents to us a man, who passes in a regular manner, over the dark and stormy sea of Generation and thus, at length, arrives at that region where tempests and seas are unknown, and finds a nation who
>
> Ne'er knew salt, or heard the billows roar.
>
> Indeed, he who is conscious of the delusions of the present life and the enchantments of this material house, in which his soul is detained, like Ulysses in the irriguous cavern of Calypso, will, like himself, continually bewail his captivity, and inly pine for a return to his native country.[3]

[1] *The Marriage of Heaven and Hell. Blake's Poetry and Prose* ed. Keynes, p. 199. Thomas Vaughan writes of the nether stars in his paraphrase of the Smaragdine Table:

> Heaven above, heaven beneath,
> Stars above, stars beneath,
> That is above is also beneath:
> Understand all this and be happy.

[2] Proclus' *Hymn to the Sun,* tr. Taylor.

[3] Taylor: Note on Plotinus, *Concerning the Beautiful.*

Earth's Answer, from 'the darkness dread and drear', describes just such a situation as that of Ulysses—*imprisoned* in a cave or *den* on a *watery shore*; and 'inly pining' for home.

> Prison'd on wat'ry shore,
> Starry Jealousy doth keep my den.

'A den with Plato, as a cavern with Empedocles, signifies, as it appears to me, this visible universe.'[1] Thus, Earth's strange landscape, of a *prison* and a *den* on a *watery shore* is entirely consistent—and consistent only—in terms of the symbolic vocabulary of Plotinus, who farther writes that Plato 'condemns the commerce of soul with body; asserting that it is confined in bonds, and buried in the body as in a sepulchre. He likewise venerates the saying which is delivered in the arcana of the sacred mysteries, that the soul is placed here *as in a prison, secured by a guard.*'[2]

The landscape and situation of Earth will be recognized as almost identical with that Oothoon in her sea-girt cave in *Visions of the Daughters of Albion*—a landscape that is also directly based upon Minutius Felix's version of the Rape of Persephone quoted by Taylor. Persephone, as she was gathering tender flowers, in the new spring, was ravished from her delightful abode by Pluto; and being carried from thence . . . *over a length of sea*, was brought by Pluto *into a cavern*. . . .[3]

[1] Plotinus: *On the Descent of Souls.*

[2] Ibid. Italics mine.

[3] An unused plate engraved for *Songs of Experience* shows the regeneration of Earth. The goddess here represented is hermaphrodite. Blake may have had other reasons for so representing the regenerate soul—Boehme, for example, declares that unfallen man, before Eve was taken from Adam's side, contained within himself both sexes. The Orphic Hymn to Zeus describes

The personification *Starry Jealousy* is an early appearance of Blake's demiurge Urizen. The allusion to the Jealous God of the Old Testament ('For I the Lord thy God am a Jealous God, visiting the sins of the fathers upon the children' etc.) is unmistakable. Starry Jealousy is the framer of the Law of Ten Commandments, the law of this world. It is he who binds the soul in her prison, seeking to impose his stony law on Love itself, who is the first of all things, the orphic Phanes and the Divine Being according to the New Testament. Is Starry Jealousy the same as

> The Holy Word
> That walk'd among the ancient trees,
>
> Calling the lapsed Soul,
> And weeping in the evening dew

I think not; the God with whom unfallen Adam conversed among the ancient trees of Eden, whom Blake describes as *weeping* because fallen man (the lapsed soul) will no longer come willingly into his presence, is not Starry Jealousy. The name *Jealousy* is Mosaic; but the epithet *Starry* identifies him, also, with the classical Demiurge as ruler of destiny. He is called Starry because he rules the stars—that is, the planetary rulers of fate.

An account of the Demiurge as the ruler of the seven planet-

---

the supreme God as bisexual. But he may also have had in mind a passage from Taylor already quoted, that describes the soul as descending as a virgin (corically) and freeing itself as a Hercules. In any case, this bisexual symbol of the perfected soul is not in any way surprising, and consistent with all the traditions known to Blake.

ary spirits (himself as the galaxy or eighth, presides over the firmament of the fixed stars, the eighth sphere) occurs in a book that Blake was almost certainly reading at this time [1] for one can trace many of his symbolic themes to this source, Everard's seventeenth-century translation of *The Divine Pymander*, attributed to Hermes Trismegistus. The ruler of the stars (of the *ogdoad*) is not the highest God, but a second god, subordinate to the first, to whom was allotted the task of creating this, the material, world, according to the model of the real, or archetypal, world:

> For the Mind being God, Male and Female, Life and Light, brought forth by his word another Mind, the Workman: Which being God of the Fire, and the Spirit, fashioned and formed seven other Governors, which in their Circles contain the Sensible World, whose Government or Disposition is called Fate or Destiny.

These are the seven planetary spirits, also described under their Greek names as the mundane gods of the Orphic Hymns—and so also known to Blake, through Taylor. The Pymander likewise says that 'the Workman mind', 'containing the Circles and whirling them about, turned round as a Wheel his own Workmanships, and suffered them to be turned from an indefinite beginning to an undeterminable End'. Blake's Urizen [2] is called 'Prince of the Starry Wheels', and ruler of

[1] See *The Tyger*.

[2] The name Urizen is derived, as Dorothy Plowman observed from 'οὐρίζειν, meaning to bound, or limit, with the cognate form Uranus, signifying the Lord of the Firmament', and not, as less learned dabblers in Blake like to pretend from 'your reason'. It is time that Mrs. Plowman's derivation be accepted once for all as the correct one.

destiny. He revolves the zodiac of the fixed stars, and the seven circles of the planets, like a wheel whose centre is 'the starry pole'. But this demiurge is not *The Holy Word*: for the Word is the Logos, Christ, or (Blake would naturally think in Swedenborgian terms) God as man, the Divine Humanity. If Blake wrote the Word, he meant precisely that—the Logos. The Holy Word and Starry Jealousy are contrasted—a deeply considered distinction that reflects Blake's belief, that he expressed long after, 'Thinking as I do that the Creator of this World is a very Cruel Being, & being a Worshipper of Christ, I cannot help saying: "the Son, O how unlike the Father". First God Almighty comes with a Thump on the Head. Then Jesus Christ comes with a balm to heal it'.[1]

Blake may have been drawing upon a number of sources. He has been called a Gnostic—partly no doubt because of an entry in Crabb Robinson's diary that describes Blake as expounding the views of the Gnostics. Perhaps he did know something of the Gnostics; Mosheim's *Ecclesiastical History* and Joseph Priestley's *An History of Early Opinions Concerning Jesus Christ* would acquaint him with the confused second-hand account of the few fragments of the Gnostics preserved by their enemies the early Church Fathers. Blake could not have read any Gnostic document—the Bruce Codex lay untranslated in the Bodleian. But the superimposition of Neoplatonism upon the Swedenborgian concept of the Divine Humanity produced something very like it, in fact a Platonized Christianity re-created from its component elements. The *Pymander*, which is not a Gnostic text, but contains many similar elements, Blake did know. The phrase *The Holy Word* is used, in the *Pymander*, in a sense that is exactly that in which Blake uses

[1] *A Vision of the Last Judgment*, *Blake's Poetry and Prose* ed. Keynes, p. 844.

it in the *Introduction*, as a manifestation of God higher than the demiurge who created this world.

With trepidation I venture to attempt an explication of knowledge that lies so far beyond the range of the lapsed soul sunk in Platonic amnesia. Briefly, the Second Book of the *Pymander* describes a vision of the narrator (Hermes Trismegistus):

'Methought I saw one of an exceeding great stature, and an infinite greatness call me by my name.' This is the Divine Pymander; and his nature is the same as that of Blake's Divine Humanity, for he is the indwelling God within the soul. This is the mystery that he reveals to Hermes: 'I am that Light, the Mind, thy God, who am before that Moist Nature that appeareth out of Darkness, and that Bright and Lightful Word from the Mind is the Son of God.' He is the Word, and the Son of God, indwelling in the soul: 'Understand it, that which in thee Seeth and Heareth, the Word of the Lord, and the Mind, the Father, God, Differeth not One from the Other, and the Unison of these is Life.' He then commands Hermes to 'conceive well the light in thy mind and know it. When he had thus said, for a long time we looked steadfastly one upon the other, in so much that I trembled at his Idea or Form.' This Holy Word was in being before the natural world was created.[1] 'Hast thou seen in thy mind that Archetypal Form, which was before the indeterminated and Infinite Beginning?'

The natural world is an imitation of the archetypal world

[1] By *before*, in texts of this kind, as with Platonism, one must understand not temporal precedence, but priority of being; as in the Gospel of St. John, *In the beginning* means in the origin, or source of things, not 'at the beginning of time'.

that has its true being as God beholds it in the Word; for 'the Mind being God . . . brought forth by his Word *another Mind, the Workman*'; but Man is the Child of the highest God.

If Blake had at this time read Robert Fludd's *Mosaicall Philosophy* (1659) he would have found there an exposition of Christian Cabbalism that identifies Christ son of the highest godhead as 'the eternal wisdom or divine Word', and goes on to say:

> 'In Christ are all things made and created. He is before all, and all, as well visible and invisible, consists in him.'

But the natural world is created by a third divine Person, the Elohim Ruach, and, here again, seven subsidiary creator-spirits, the seven lower Sefiroth.

Fludd's Elohim Ruach has many of the characteristics of Blake's Urizen, and is certainly one of the models from which that impressive and familiar figure is drawn. One word, in *Earth's Answer*, makes it seem not improbable that Blake had at this time already read Fludd; for Earth addresses Starry Jealousy as

> Selfish father of men!
> Cruel, jealous selfish *fear*.

Now Fludd writes of the Elohim who with his sons creates the elemental world, 'This name Elohim, according to the Cabbalistical interpretation, *doth signifie fear, and terror*' [1]. I do not know where, otherwise, Blake could have found the attribute *fear* here assigned to the Demiurge. It is not, after all, one that is at all obvious.

[1] *Mosaicall Philosophy*: italics mine.

Whatever, then, may have been Blake's sources, there seems little doubt that the Holy Word, and Starry Jealousy, are, respectively, the Logos, and the Demiurge of the natural world—also a manifestation of Deity, but of an ambiguous, indeed in part an evil, nature; as he appears in Blake's later writings as Urizen, ruler of the stars and of destiny.

The syntax of the first verses of the *Introduction* is profoundly ambiguous; nor does Blake's own erratic punctuation, which I have here restored, help in any way:

> Hear the voice of the Bard.
> Who Present, Past & Future, sees
> Whose ears have heard,
> The Holy Word,
> That walk'd among the ancient trees.
>
> Calling the lapsed Soul
> And weeping in the evening dew:
> The might controll
> The starry pole;
> And fallen, fallen light renew!

Who is it

> That might controll
> The starry pole?

Is it *the voice of the Bard, the Holy Word,* or *the lapsed Soul*? All readings make sense. The voice of the Bard is the voice of imagination; and for Blake the voice of imagination is the voice of Jesus (the Word), as might be proved from any number of passages, in which Jesus and the Imagination are used synonymously. The Holy Word is the Divine Logos, Jesus himself, God as manifested to man, and within man. Adam unfallen in the Garden of Eden communed continually with this divine presence. If it is *the lapsed Soul* herself who 'might controll the starry pole', this also would be true because the Divine Humanity dwells within the soul, whose own nature is divine: 'We are all coexistent with God, Members of the Divine body. We are all partakers of the divine nature.' [1] Can it be that Blake intentionally left the syntax ambiguous, feeling, as he read the poem over, that it said exactly what he wanted to say, without further alteration?

Unfallen man—Adam walking in Eden hearing the voice of God; the Platonic soul before she enters the Kingdom of Pluto and the rule of the planetary governors, through the Northern Gate of the Zodiac—are not subject to the rule of Starry Jealousy. The tyranny of the Demiurge of the natural world has no power over the awakened soul, 'that might controll the starry pole' if she could, in the Platonic language, remember again what in her sleep she has forgotten—her divine nature.

One still unexplained figure is the Bard. Perhaps he needs little explanation. In the *Songs of Experience* the Bard appears twice, in both contexts announcing the return of the eternal day.

In *The Voice of the Ancient Bard* the call to awakening is answered:

> Youth of delight come hither,
> And see the opening morn,
> Image of truth new born.

[1] *Blake, Coleridge, Wordsworth, Lamb, etc. being selections from the Remains of Henry Crabb Robinson* ed. Edith J. Morley (Manchester V.P., 1922), p. 3.

But in Blake's later writings the term *Bard* is discarded in favour of *Prophet* or *Poetic Imagination.* An obvious source of the earlier *Bard* is Gray, whose poems Blake much admired, and illustrated [1] at about this time. Both Blake's political and his religious condemnation of the tyrant are echoed in the opening lines spoken by Gray's *Bard*:

> Ruin seize thee, ruthless King!
> Confusion on thy banners wait,
> Tho' fann'd by Conquest's crimson wing
> They mock the air with idle state.
> Helm, nor Hauberk's twisted mail,
> Nor even thy virtues, Tyrant, shall avail . . .

If one reads these lines as if addressed to Starry Jealousy, one sees why Gray's fierce Bard must have been a sympathetic figure to Blake. The last line—the unavailing power of the *virtues* of the Tyrant—might almost be a summary of the judgment Blake passed upon Urizen and 'the selfish virtues of the natural heart' that he sought, by his morality, to instil. But this is to anticipate. The figure of Urizen is here present only in its embryonic form.

[1] Probably in 1793–4.

II

William Blake, Isaac Watts, and Mrs. Barbauld

by

V. de S. Pinto
The University of Nottingham (*Great Britain*)

II

William Blake, Isaac Watts, and Mrs. Barbauld

SEVERAL CRITICS[1] HAVE noticed that Blake's *Songs of Innocence and Experience* were influenced by Dr. Isaac Watts's *Divine Songs attempted in Easy Language for the use of Children*, but the relationship between the work of the two authors has never been explored in detail. The following notes are suggestions which may serve as a starting point for such an exploration.

Isaac Watts, the celebrated nonconformist divine, poet, and educationalist of the early eighteenth century, was a man who stood between two worlds. As an Independent preacher, he was the inheritor of the old Calvinist tradition of rigid morality and bibliolatry. Yet he was also a humanist of the reign of Queen Anne with a classical education and a philosophic training, a student of Descartes and Locke, of Milton, Pope, and Addison. His whole career is built on a compromise between the old Puritanism of the age of Cromwell and the new humanism of the age of Addison.

William Blake, the poor, self-educated London engraver, also belongs to the Puritan tradition. His family was nonconformist, but Puritanism had by now undergone a remarkable change. The old legalistic Calvinism was in a much more advanced state of decay than in Watts's time, and the rigid morality, already softening in Queen Anne's reign, was now in full retreat before the armies of free thought and revolutionary

[1] See S. Foster Damon, *William Blake his Philosophy and Symbols*, p. 41; Mona Wilson, *The Life of William Blake*, p. 38; A. P. Davis, *Isaac Watts his Life and Works* (New York, 1943), p. 228.

speculation. Blake was an open rebel, where Watts was only a mild critic, and many passages in Blake's works show that the compromise which Watts suavely maintained throughout his life has now been flung to the winds.

> I went to the Garden of Love,
> And saw what I never had seen:
> A Chapel was built in the midst,
> Where I used to play on the green.
>
> And the gates of this Chapel were shut,
> And 'Thou shall not' writ over the door;
> So I turn'd to the Garden of Love;
> That so many sweet flowers bore;
>
> And I saw it was filled with graves,
> And tomb-stones where flowers should be;
> And Priests in black gowns were walking their rounds,
> And binding with briars my joys & desires.[1]

The revolt against traditional Puritan morality is very clearly symbolized in these lines. We can contrast them with numerous passages in Watts's writings which express the traditional Puritan condemnation of sensuality:

> It is the great business of sinners to fulfil the lusts of the flesh, and make provision for it. The things that relate to the flesh, and the enjoyments of this sensible and present life, are the objects of sinful appetites, or of lawful appetite in a sinful degree and therefore sin is called flesh. Sin is also called flesh because it is communicated and propagated to us by the parents of our flesh. It is by our flesh that we are akin to

[1] Blake, *Poetry and Prose*, ed. Keynes (1927), p. 75.

> Adam, the first great sinner, and derive a corrupted nature from him.[1]

What was sin for Watts has become the 'garden of love' for Blake; and 'Thou shalt not', which for Watts was the injunction of a beneficent creator, in Blake's poem is the command of a tyrant.

Yet in spite of this apparent contrast, which might be illustrated by many passages from the works of the two writers, there are striking resemblances between some of their most characteristic doctrines and beliefs. Both believe in poetic inspiration and prefer Hebrew to Graeco-Roman poetry;[2] both condemn 'Natural Religion and Deism'. Both believe in a God of forgiveness as opposed to a God of wrath.

Watts sometimes speaks almost in the very accents of Blake, especially when he is dealing with such subjects as inspiration and faith, and contrasting them with rationality and intellect:

> Learning and wit may cease their strife
> When miracles with glory shine;
> The voice that calls the dead to life,
> Must be almighty and divine.
>
> * * * * *
>
> Let Heathens scoff and Jews oppose
> Let Satan's bolts be hurl'd;
> There's something wrought within you shews
> That Jesus saves the world.[3]

[1] Isaac Watts, Sermon IV, *Works* (1812) I, 46.

[2] See Watts, Preface to *Horae Lyricae* (1709) *ed. cit.* IX, 222: 'The Gentiles talk and trifle upon this subject, when brought into comparison with Moses, whom Longinus . . . cites as a master of the sublime style.' Cf. Blake, Preface to *Milton*: 'The Stolen & Perverted writings of Homer & Ovid . . . are set up by artifice against the Sublime of the Bible.'

[3] Watts, *ed. cit.*, I, 44.

Blake may well have had these lines in mind when he wrote his famous protests against rationalism and its child, imperialism:

> Mock on, Mock on Voltaire, Rousseau:
> Mock on, Mock on: 'tis all in vain!
> You throw the sand against the wind,
> And the wind blows back it again.[1]

> Titus! Constantine! Charlemaine!
> O Voltaire! Rousseau! Gibbon! Vain
> Your Grecian Mocks & Roman Sword
> Against this image of his Lord! [2]

One of the earliest reviews of Blake's poetry (in the *Monthly Review* for October, 1806) compares him with Watts as a poet of childhood, and, among later critics, Foster Damon and Mona Wilson have both made passing allusions to Blake's debt to Watts in *The Songs of Innocence* and *Experience*. Watts's *Divine Songs for Children* was one of the most popular books of the eighteenth century. As Mr. A. P. Davis has shown in his study of Watts,[3] it is the inheritor of the tradition of the numerous Puritan 'good godly books' for children published in the seventeenth century, but Watts's collection gave an entirely new tone to the poetry of childhood. Though much of it seems to us now merely versified moralizing, there is a lyrical charm in the best of Watts's child poems, which was quite unknown to the old Puritan versifiers. Moreover, Watts was a forward-

[1] Blake, *ed. cit.*, p. 107. [2] Blake, *ed. cit.*, p. 649.
[3] A. P. Davis, *op. cit.*, Ch. IV.

looking poet. In the short preface to the 'Slight Specimen of Moral Songs' which he appends to the *Divine Songs* he writes that they are 'such as I wish some happy and condescending Genius would undertake for the use of children, and perform much better'.

Robert Graves once gave a specimen of what he called 'a formal version logicalized in creaking sonnet form' of Blake's 'Infant Joy':

> But thou, Blest Infant, smiling radiantly
> Hast taught me . . .[1]

He suggests also that 'an immoral but far more entertaining parlour game than logicalization . . . would be to extract the essentials from some long-winded but sincere Augustan poem, disguise the self-conscious antitheses, modernize the diction, liven up the rhythm, fake a personal twist, and publish'. Mr. Graves was not apparently aware of the fact that Blake himself (perhaps unconsciously) did something very much like what he suggested as a parlour game for a modern poet. Watts's masterpiece of child poetry, the famous 'Cradle Hymn', which stands at the end of his *Moral Songs*, is a very good Augustan poem (hardly long-winded, certainly sincere, and not, perhaps, free from self-conscious antithesis). Blake's 'Cradle Song' in the *Songs of Innocence* might be described as a 'delogicalization' of Watts's poem, to which Blake has given a rhythm akin to, yet differing from, that of the original, and a very distinct 'personal twist'. It is instructive to place the two poems side by side.

[1] Robert Graves, *On English Poetry* (1922), pp. 67, 68.

A Cradle Hymn [1] (Isaac Watts)

Hush! my dear, lie still and slumber;
Holy angels guard thy bed!
Heavenly blessings without number
Gently falling on thy head.

2

Sleep, my babe; thy food and raiment,
House and home thy friends provide,
All without thy care or payment,
All thy wants are well supply'd.

3

How much better thou'rt attended
Than the Son of God could be,
When from heaven he descended
And became a child like thee.

4

Soft and easy is thy cradle;
Coarse and hard thy Saviour lay;
When his birthplace was a stable,
And his softest bed was hay,

5

Blessed babe! what glorious features,
Spotless fair, divinely bright!
Must he dwell with brutal creatures?
How could angels bear the sight?

6

Was there nothing but a manger
Cursed sinners could afford,
To receive the heav'nly stranger?
Did they thus affront their Lord?

A Cradle Song [2] (William Blake)

Sweet dreams, form a shade
O'er my lovely infant's head
Sweet dreams of pleasant streams
By happy, silent, moony beams.

2

Sweet sleep, with soft down
Weave thy brows an infant crown,
Sweet sleep, Angel mild
Hover o'er my happy child.

3

Sweet smiles, in the night
Hover over my delight.
Sweet smiles, Mother's smiles,
All the livelong night beguiles.

4

Sweet moans, dovelike sighs,
Chase not slumber from thy eyes.
Sweet moans, sweeter smiles,
All the dovelike moans beguiles.

5

Sleep, sleep, happy child,
All creation slept and smil'd
Sleep, sleep, happy sleep,
While o'er thee thy mother weep.

6

Sweet babe in thy face,
Holy image I can trace.
Sweet babe, once like thee,
Thy maker lay and wept for me,

[1] Isaac Watts, *ed. cit.*, X, 26.

[2] Blake, *ed. cit.*, pp. 61, 62.

7

Soft, my child; I did not chide thee,
Tho' my song might sound too hard:
Tis thy mother sits besides thee,
And her arm shall be thy guard.

8

Yet to read the shameful story,
How the Jews abused their King,
How they serv'd the Lord of glory,
Makes me angry while I sing.

9

See the kinder shepherds round him
Telling wonders from the sky:
There they sought him, there they
found him.
With his virgin Mother by.

10

See the lovely Babe a dressing:
Lovely Infant, how he smil'd!
When he wept the Mother's bless-
ing
Sooth'd and hush'd the holy Child.

11

Lo, he slumbers in his manger,
Where the horned oxen feed;
Peace, my darling, here's no danger,
Here's no ox anear thy bed.

12

'Twas to save thee, child, from dy-
ing,
Save my dear from burning flame,
Bitter groans, and endless crying,
That thy blest Redeemer came.

7

Wept for me, for thee, for all,
When he was an infant small.
Thou his image ever see,
Heavenly face that smiles on thee,

8

Smiles on thee, on me, on all;
Who became an infant small.
Infant smiles are his own smiles
Heaven & earth to peace beguiles.

13

Mays't thou live to know and fear
him,
Trust and love him all thy days!
Then go dwell for ever near him,
See his face and sing his praise!

14

I could give thee thousand kisses,
Hoping what I most desire;
Not a mother's fondest wishes,
Can to greater joys aspire.

The general schemes of the two poems are very similar. Both begin with the lulling of the child to sleep and the calling down of 'blessings' (Watts) or 'sweet dreams' (Blake) on its head. 'Head' in this connection is a rime word in both opening stanzas. Angels are called upon to guard Watts's child and the Angel Sleep to hover over Blake's. In both poems the human child is compared with the Christ-child. In stanza 3 of Watts's poem Christ is said to become 'a child *like thee*' and in stanza 6 of Blake's poem we find a line ending with the same words: 'Sweet babe, once *like thee*.' The words 'infant' and 'smile' (smiles—smil'd) are used in connection with the Christ-child in stanza 7 of Blake's poem and in stanza 10 of Watts's. In stanza 13 of Watts's poem the human child is exhorted to see the face of Christ and in stanza 7 of Blake's almost the same words are used.

The differences between the poems are as interesting as the resemblances. Watts's poem is classical in its clarity, its logical development and its sharp outlines. The comparison between the human child and the Christ-child is emphasized by means of a series of antitheses. These are followed by the rhetorical questions which bring out the contrast between the glory of Christ and the meanness of his reception on earth, with an effective pause in the declamation to reassure the human child. The allusion to the coming tragedy of the crucifixion leads up to the detailed description of the Christ-child in the traditional surroundings visualized as clearly as in a painting of the Italian renaissance. Blake uses the same material, but eliminates all the rhetoric and all the description. He has translated Watts's poem, as it were, into a new poetic idiom.

Both poems are in four-accent lines with a falling ('trochaic') rhythm arranged in four-line stanzas—Watts's lines rime alternately, Blake's in couplets. Watts's rhythm (helped by his double rimes) is bold and flowing, Blake's is much subtler, a sort of croon, swaying, as it were, gently to and fro like a cradle. This effect is achieved by the frequent and masterly use of monosyllabic feet in place of the complete falling foot or 'trochee':

/ / / × /
Sweet dreams, form a shade. . . .
/ / × / × /
Sweet dreams of pleasant streams.

Watts's characteristic device is antithesis, Blake's repetition. Watts's poem appeals to the intellect and the visual imagination; Blake's is a sort of incantation, where the emotive value of words is the chief consideration, to which even grammar is sacrificed (as in stanzas 3 and 4). In Watts's poem the divine child is quite separate from the human child, and is, indeed, contrasted with him. His surroundings (the shepherds, the manger, and the horned oxen) are described, and his death is foretold. In the twelfth stanza there is even a statement of orthodox dogma. All these details disappear in Blake's poems. The divine child is partly blended with the human child; he is a 'holy image', which the poet can see in the baby's face. His sufferings are only mentioned in a few words, and he is conceived as a 'heavenly face' which in some mysterious way the human child sees smiling, and which is identified with the smiling face of all human children.

The flower poem, the animal or bird poem, and the insect poem are all traditional features of collections of children's poetry in the seventeenth and eighteenth centuries and were derived, doubtless, from the old Emblem books. All these types are found both in Watts and Blake, as well as in earlier collections such as Bunyan's *Book for Boys and Girls*. It is interesting to examine the treatment of the insect theme in poems by Bunyan, Watts and Blake respectively. Bunyan, basing his poem on *Proverbs*, VI, 6–8, regards the insect simply as an object lesson in the Puritan virtues of thrift and prudence:

> Must we unto the pismire go to school,
> To learn of her in summer to provide
> For winter next ensuing. Man's a fool,
> Or silly ants would not be made his guide.
> But, sluggard, is it not a shame for thee
> To be outdone by pismires? [1]

Watts also uses the ant as a text for a versified sermon, but, unlike Bunyan, he takes some interest in the insects for their own sake; in the first three lines of his poem he expresses the imaginative appeal of their smallness and helplessness.

[1] Bunyan, *A Book for Boys and Girls*, No. XXIII, *Collected Works*, ed. Offor (1867), III, p. 758.

These Emmets, how little they seem in our eyes!
We tread them to dust, and a troop of them dies,
Without our regard or concern: . . .[1]

The rest of the poem is mere moralizing, but the opening lines suggest an entirely new way of treating the subject. Blake took his cue from Watts. His poem 'The Dream' [2] is a vision of the smallness and helplessness of the insect world. The moralizing has entirely disappeared.

Once a dream did weave a shade
O'er my Angel-guarded bed,
That an Emmet lost its way
Where on grass methought I lay.

Troubled, 'wilder'd and forlorn,
Dark, benighted, travel-worn,
Over many a tangled spray,
All heart-broke I heard her say:

'O my children! do they cry?
Do they hear their father sigh?
Now they look abroad to see;
Now return to weep for me.'

Bunyan writes about a single pismire, but his insect is only an abstraction standing for Puritan virtue. Watts can only think of his emmets in the mass, but he can appreciate the poetic value of their smallness, as well as their convenience as object

[1] Watts, *ed. cit.*, IX, p. 215. [2] Blake, *ed. cit.*, p. 52.

lessons for the moralist. Blake, like Bunyan, deals with a single emmet, but for him the insect is not an allegory of thrift or prudence at all, but an image of smallness, loneliness and bewilderment. Perhaps a comparison between the three poems has a wider significance. They represent three different stages in the approach of adults to the world of childhood (for the insect is the symbol of the child). In Bunyan we see the adult interested only in forcing the child into the mould of a traditional morality. Watts also holds this view, as it were officially, but he has a secret sympathy for the child as a child, and feels the charm and beauty of the small and the helpless. Blake no longer thinks of turning the child into a model of adult virtue, but tries to enter with imaginative sympathy into the child-world of smallness, helplessness and bewilderment.

Some of Blake's *Songs of Experience* seem like direct answers to Watts's *Divine Songs*. For instance, No. XXIII of Watts's collection is a sort of versified gloss on the fifth commandment. 'Children that would fear the Lord' are told to listen to their teachers and obey their parents 'with reverence and delight'. Dreadful things are threatened

> To him that breaks his father's law,
> Or mocks his mother's word.

'Heavy guilt' is said to lie upon him. His name is to be cursed. Ravens are to pick out his eyes, 'and eagles eat the same'. Blake's 'A Little Boy Lost' in *Songs of Experience* is surely intended as a reply to this fierce Old Testament morality. In the two opening quatrains Blake seems to be trying to express the sort of reasoning with which a child might be made to answer such precepts as these of Watts:

Nought loves another as itself,
  Nor venerates another so,
Nor is it possible to Thought
  A greater than itself to know:

And Father, how can I love you
  Or any of my brothers more?
I love you like the little bird
  That picks up crumbs around the door.

Blake imagines a 'priest' overhearing these words, seizing the child by the hair, stripping him to his 'little shirt', and binding him with an iron chain. Then they

  burn'd him in a holy place,
Where many had been burn'd before: . . .

Surely this 'holy place' is the place where Watts's ravens and eagles peck out the dead child's eyes. Both poems are symbols of the killing of the child-mind by the spirit of Puritan morality. Watts, with all his sensibility, regards the sacrifice as part of the divine plan; for Blake it is a murder, which evokes the horrified question: 'Are such things done on Albion's shore?' [1]

Both Watts and Blake were concerned with the relationship of the child to poverty. Blake's famous poem 'London' in *The Songs of Experience* is, I believe, connected with Song IV of Watts's collection. If the poems are placed side by side, it will be seen that the relationship between them is not unlike that between 'A Cradle Hymn' and 'A Cradle Song'. There are

[1] Blake, *ed. cit.*, p. 78.

indeed no close verbal resemblances between these poems, and nothing could be more unlike the smugness of Watts's poem than the tragic intensity of Blake's, but the sequence of ideas in the two poems is the same. Both begin with a walk through the town. In both, the vision of poverty and misery follows, and in both the vision is completed by a picture of the foul-mouthed children of eighteenth-century London. Again Blake is more succinct that Watts. He suppresses the moralizing of Watts's child and the rhetorical antitheses, and in place of Watts's vague generalizations, gives us the terribly distinct images of the child chimney sweep, the 'black'ning church', the 'youthful harlot' and the 'marriage hearse'.

Isaac Watts. Song IV
(*Divine Songs for Children*)

Whene'er I take my walks abroad,
  How many poor I see,
What shall I render to my God
  For all his gifts to me?

Not more than others I deserve,
  Yet God hath given me more;
For I have food while others starve,
  Or beg from door to door.

How many children in the street
  Half naked I behold!
While I am clothed from head to feet,
  And covered from the cold.

While some poor wretches scarce can tell
  Where they may lay their head:
I have a home wherein to dwell,
  And rest upon my bed.

William Blake. 'London'
(*Songs of Experience*)

I wander thro' each charter'd street,
Near where the charter'd Thames does flow,
And mark in every face I meet
Marks of weekness, marks of woe.

In every cry of every Man,
In every Infant's cry of fear,
In every voice, in every ban,
The mind-forg'd manacles I hear.

How the Chimney-sweeper's cry
Every black'ning Church appalls;
And the hopeless Soldier's sigh
Runs in blood down Palace walls.

While others early learn to swear,
And curse and lye, and steal;
Lord, I am taught thy name to fear,
And do thy holy will.

Are these thy favours, day by day
To me above the rest?
Then let me love thee more than they,
And try to serve thee best.

But most thro' midnight streets I hear
How the youthful Harlot's curse
Blasts the new born Infant's tear,
And blights with plagues the Marriage hearse.

Blake's two Holy Thursday poems were apparently suggested by a Charity School service at St. Paul's. Watts published an *Essay on Charity Schools* in 1723; and the similarity of a passage in this Essay to the second Holy Thursday poem suggests to me that Blake had read it. Watts's *Essay* exhibits a characteristic dualism of thought. On the one hand he feels a generous sympathy with the poor child and a desire to give it education. On the other hand he is a firm supporter of the social structure of contemporary England, and entirely agrees with such writers as Bishop Edmund Gibson, who contended that Charity Schools ought not to teach such 'polite' subjects as Latin, Greek, modern languages and mathematics, which were only suitable for young ladies and gentlemen.[1] To those critics of Charity Schools who argued that poor children ought to be brought up to be servants and that education would make them 'high, haughty and wasteful', Watts replies that the sort of education that Charity Schools gave would make them more useful as servants and at the same time better Christians. This is his main argument, but it is qualified in several places by the writer's liberal and humane spirit. He puts in a plea for the 'lad of bright genius' who may be found here and there among the poor. 'Diamonds of a noble lustre are taken from common

[1] Quoted by Watts, *ed. cit.*, VI, 28.

earth, and every diamond is rough or cloudy, till it is polished. If there is a vein of silver mixed with the leaden ore, why should it be denied the favour of the refining-pot, since nature seems to have made it on purpose to shine and glitter'? [1]

There is a glow of generous indignation in the passage in which Watts dwells on the unhappy condition of children of parents who have lost their money and who, after enjoying wealth and ease, are reduced to the humiliations of poverty. I believe that Blake had this passage in mind when he wrote the second Holy Thursday poem in *Songs of Experience*.

Isaac Watts
'An Essay on Charity Schools (1723)' [2]

Yet surely there may be some exceptions made for the children of those poor parents, who have enjoyed plentiful circumstances in life, and have behaved well in them, and performed the duties of justice and charity; but by the wise providence of God have been reduced to great degrees of poverty, and are hardly able to provide food and clothing for their own offspring, and much less to bestow a good education upon them. Some of these children are yet sunk deeper into distress, and are become orphans. Such misery has somewhat of a sacred tenderness belonging to it, and seems to claim the regards of sympathy and compassion from those who enjoy plentiful circumstances, while they meditate on the uncertainty of human affairs, and remember they are liable to the like calamity.

William Blake. 'Holy Thursday' [3]

Is this a holy thing to see
In a rich and fruitful land,
Babes reduc'd to misery,
Fed with cold and usurous hand?

Is that trembling cry a song?
Can it be a song of joy?
And so many children poor?
It is a land of poverty!

And their sun does never shine,
And their fields are bleak & bare,
And their ways are fill'd with thorns:
It is eternal winter there.

For wher-e'er the sun does shine,
And wher-e'er the rain does fall
Babe can never hunger there,
Nor poverty the mind appall.

[1] Watts, *An Essay on Charity Schools, ed. cit.*, VI, p. 12.

[2] Watts, *ibid.*, p. 9.

[3] Blake, *ed. cit.*, pp. 70, 71.

It can hardly be an accident that the key words 'reduced' and 'poverty' occur both in the prose passage and in the poem. The last sentence of the prose passage may be connnected with the last line of Blake's first 'Holy Thursday' poem in *The Songs of Innocence*: 'Then cherish pity, lest you drive an angel from your door.'

A study of the relationship between the writings of Watts and Blake, is not merely an exploration of literary sources. It throws light on an important phase of the development both of poetic sensibility and of the social conscience.

A contemporary of Blake, Mrs. Anna Letitia Barbauld, published in 1781 a little book which seems to have been planned as a sort of supplement to, or, perhaps, a substitute for Watts's *Divine Songs for Children*. This pamphlet of ninety-eighty pages called *Hymns in Prose for Children* [1] was published anonymously by Joseph Johnson of 72, St. Paul's Churchyard, the publisher of Wordsworth's first volume of poems, to whose circle we know that the young Blake belonged.[2] Mrs. Barbauld is also said to have been an acquaintance of Mrs. Mathew at whose parties Blake used to read his early poems.[3] It is, therefore, highly probable that Blake knew Mrs. Barbauld's *Hymns in Prose*.

Mrs. Barbauld's purpose is didactic and religious. In her Preface she complains that, though there are many books which 'unfold the system and give a summary of the doctrines of religion' for children, 'it would be difficult to find one calculated to assist them in the devotional part of it, except indeed

[1] *Hymns in Prose for Children by the Author of Lessons for Children.* London. Printed for J. Johnson. MDCCLXXXI.

[2] See Mona Wilson, *The Life of William Blake* (1948), pp. 41, 42.

[3] Mona Wilson, *op. cit.*, p. 18.

Dr. Watts's *Hymns for Children*. 'These', she continues, 'are in pretty general use and the author is deservedly honoured for the condescension of his Muse which was very able to take a loftier flight. But it may very well be doubted, whether poetry *ought* to be lowered to the capacities of children, or whether they should not rather be kept from reading verse, till they are able to relish good verse: for the very essence of poetry is an elevation in thought and style above the common standard; and if it wants this character, it wants all that renders it valuable.' It may be noticed incidentally that the last sentence represents precisely the view of poetry that Wordsworth was soon to combat so memorably and Mrs. Barbauld's words may well have been in his mind when he composed the famous Advertizement to the first edition of *Lyrical Ballads*.

Mrs. Barbauld may be described not unfairly as a talented, pious prig. Her *Hymns in Prose* are entirely conventional in sentiment and are written in a pseudo-biblical style with many echoes of the Authorized Version of the Psalms and other parts of the Bible. They almost certainly suggested images and phrases to Blake, and a few examples will show how he transmuted Mrs. Barbauld's tinsel into the gold of authentic poetry. In Hymn III she describes a shepherd with the help of reminiscences of Psalm XXIII: 'Behold the shepherd of the flock, he taketh care of his sheep, he leadeth them among clear brooks, he guideth them to fresh pasture; if the young lambs are weary, he carrieth them in his arms; if they wander, he bringeth them back.' [1] This passage may well be the germ of Blake's 'The Shepherd':

[1] Mrs. Barbauld, *op. cit.*, pp. 12, 13.

How sweet is the Shepherd's sweet lot!
From the morn till the evening he strays;
He shall follow his sheep all the day,
And his tongue shall be filled with praise.

For he hears the lambs' innocent call,
And he hears the ewes' tender reply;
He is watchful while they are in peace,
For they know that their Shepherd is nigh.[1]

The opening sentences of Mrs. Barbauld's Hymn V probably gave Blake a hint for the opening stanza of 'Night':

'The glorious sun is set in the West; the nightdews fall; and the air which was sultry, becomes cool. The flowers fold up their coloured leaves; they fold themselves up, and hang their heads on their slender stalks.' [2]

The sun descending in the West,
The evening star does shine;
The birds are silent in their nest,
And I must seek for mine.
The moon like a flower
In heaven's high bower,
With silent delight
Sits and smiles at the night.[3]

Mrs. Barbauld does not mention the moon, but Blake's exquisite image of the flower may well have been suggested by the

[1] Blake's *Prose and Poetry, ed. cit.*, p. 59.
[2] Mrs. Barbauld, *op. cit.*, pp. 25, 26.
[3] Blake, *ed. cit.*, p. 60.

prose passage. One of the greatest lyrics in *The Songs of Experience* was possibly suggested by two passages in Mrs. Barbauld's *Hymns*. In Hymn IX she asks a rhetorical question about the flowers: 'How doth the rose draw its crimson from the dark brown earth, or the lily its shining white?'[1] In Hymn X she speaks of the decay of the rose: 'I have seen the rose in its beauty; it spread its leaves to the morning sun—I returned, it was dying upon its stalk; the grace of the form of it was gone; its loveliness was vanished away; the leaves thereof were scattered to the ground and no one gathered them again.'[2] Elements from these two passages seem to be combined in 'The Sick Rose' of *Songs of Experience*:

O Rose, thou art sick!
The invisible worm.
That flies in the night
In the howling storm,

Has found out thy bed
Of crimson joy
And his dark secret love
Does thy life destroy.[3]

Mrs. Barbauld does not mention the worm in connexion with her dying rose, but, in the hymn quoted above (no. X) she goes on to describe the downfall of a 'stately tree' because 'the worm had made its way into the trunk, and the heart thereof was de-

[1] Mrs. Barbauld, *op. cit.*, p. 70.
[2] Mrs. Barbauld, *op. cit.*, pp. 77, 78.
[3] Blake, *ed. cit.*, p. 72.

cayed, it mouldered away, and fell to the ground.'[1] Blake seems to have taken the worm from Mrs. Barbauld's 'stately tree' and placed it in his Sick Rose.

The chief interest of Mrs. Barbauld's book for students of Blake lies in the fact that it is the last link in a tradition of popular poetry for children which goes back to the seventeenth century. 'Blake', writes Professor Sir Anthony Blunt, 'filled his memory with images seen in the work of other artists and used them in his own works. But he absorbed these images so completely and gave them such a strongly personal form when he reproduced them that they bear the full stamp of originality.' Sir Anthony is speaking here of Blake's designs but his words apply equally to his poetry. In *Poetical Sketches* Blake began by trying to write in the tradition of English literary poetry. When he made a fresh start in *The Songs of Innocence and Experience* (heralded by some of the songs in *An Island in the Moon*) he turned to another tradition, that of popular poetry and especially popular poetry for children. This tradition he absorbed as completely as Burns absorbed the tradition of Scottish folk-song, and, like Burns, he transmuted what he borrowed into a new and unique creation.

[1] Mrs. Barbauld, *op. cit.*, p. 79.

III

Blake and Milton

by

S. Foster Damon
Brown University, Rhode Island (*U.S.A.*)

III

Blake and Milton

LITERATURE IS BASICALLY of two types, the realistic and the symbolic. The realists are Chaucer, most of Shakspere, Fielding, Jane Austen, and the travelogues of Melville, to name a few. These works treat of individuals in human society set in a three-dimensional world. The symbolists are Dante, Spenser, Shakspere's supernatural plays (and indeed practically anything using the supernatural), Milton, Blake, Shelley, and the novels of Melville. These works deal not with men but with Man, in a psychological universe.

Blake used to be treated as a freak, a stray out of the real line of literature, simply because the symbolic line was not recognized. But the line is clear. Milton told Dryden that his 'original' was Spenser, and the scholars have since proved his constant, deep indebtedness. Blake wrote Flaxman: 'Milton lov'd me in childhood & shew'd me his face' and all through his career, Blake followed Milton.

Blake was the first person, and until our day the only one, to recognize that Milton was a symbolic poet. The great bulk of readers took *Paradise Lost* as simply an expansion of Biblical history (although it is no more history than the *Divine Comedy* is a travelogue), while the educated gentlemen admired the poem enormously as an epic constructed upon the formula of Aristotle. Blake, however, knew that Milton was trying to say 'Things unattempted yet in Prose or Rhime'; he read the stories of Satan and Adam as profound studies in the processes of

Sin; and Milton's worlds of Heaven and Hell were written anagogically about Man, who contains both.

But Blake did not copy Milton: he was inspired by him. Where Milton experimented, he carried the experiments further; and when Milton expressed an idea, Blake either attacked it or extended it to new conclusions.

He began by perceiving the secret of Milton's blank verse, and opened his *Poetical Sketches* with six examples of blank verse now first used for lyrics. The last poem in the book is a specimen of blankish, freeish verse on the subject of Samson; but he had not yet discovered the meaning of *Samson Agonistes*, for Blake's Dalila is only the agent of the Philistine lords, and not Milton's Female Will, which Blake later was to denounce so bitterly.

'L'Allegro' and 'Il Penseroso' together constitute a single, circular poem, each beginning where the other ends. The two are bound together by contrasting images: day—night, the lark—the nightingale, and so forth. They depict the alternating moods of the Puritan gentleman: innocent gaiety and serious thought. Blake expanded the idea to the 'two contrary states of the human soul', the extremes, ecstasy and despair, and bound the *Songs of Innocence* to the *Songs of Experience* by pairing his contrasted lyrics, so that each complements the other.

Not till the *Book of Thel*, however, did he really criticize one of Milton's ideas. This poem is a reconsideration of the idea on which *Comus* is based. Milton wrote it as a moral lesson for little Lady Alix Egerton, who acted the leading role in the masque. The girl is approaching womanhood. She is lost in a forest, where she hears strange voices; but she appeals to Chastity, and the virgin Moon appears, stopping the voices and lighting her path. The evil Comus disguised as an innocent shepherd inveigles her into his palace, where with his wand he fixes her in a chair and presses upon her the cup of dissipation. She has the moral strength to refuse the cup, but she cannot escape from the enchantment of his person until Sabrina (the curative forces of nature) releases her from the glamour. Thus Lady Alix learned that her first infatuation might be for an unworthy person; but if she resisted him, she would recover from the spell.

Thel is also the girl on the verge of womanhood, about to pass from Innocence into Experience. She fears the change as though it were death (for all change is death to what was). She laments the passing of her spring, then she questions successively the meaning of her own innocence (the Lily), of the male (the youthful Cloud), and of motherhood (the matron Clay with her baby Worm). All reply that they live then pass away unquestioning their divine guidance, that they find happiness in serving their purpose, and that nothing lives for itself alone.

Then Thel, through her imagination (the Northern gate), enters the realm of the matron Clay, and comes to her own grave plot (her future life in Experience). She imagines her maturity to be the grave of all her youth and beauty, in a world of lamentations. From this grave she hears the strange voices which Milton's Lady repressed so primly; they are the five senses waking to their new life. At the cry of Touch (sex), Thel shrieks and flees back to the land of her Innocence.

Thus Blake reworked the basic idea of *Comus* into a new tale, told not in moral but in biological terms. Curiously, however, Thel never reappears in his later works: the nice English girl that she is had no place in his vaster scheme. When he continued the idea in *The Visions of the Daughters of Albion*, Thel is renamed Oothoon, who is not only the woman caught in the woes of Experience, but in a larger sense is every soul which is torn between desire and duty. The Cloud reappears in *Europe* with the name Antamon, 'prince of the pearly dew'. The baby Worm, however, never acquires a name.

Thel's flight back to Innocence seems to me to be simply the girl's natural revulsion against the demands of her maturing flesh. It has usually been interpreted, however, as the soul's refusal to leave Eternity and descend into this world of generation. Now this idea could be true, as the larger and smaller patterns repeat each other. But most souls do not refuse to be born, and therefore at this point *The Book of Thel* would cease to be of universal application. Perhaps that is why Thel never reappears in the other books. Possibly the poem is at heart an elegy to a still-born child of the Blakes'. Certainly in *Jerusalem* (56: 14–16) Blake refers to a miscarriage when Los bids the Daughters of Albion weave on the loom of love a garment and a cradle for 'the infantine Terror' lest in fear 'at entering the gates into our World of cruel Lamentation, it flee back & hide in Non-Entity's dark wild'.

Once we have seen how Blake utilized Milton's ideas, the relationship of their works is much more apparent.

The Visions of the Daughters of Albion corresponds to the divorce books. Both attack the unhappy marriage; but where Milton is content to advocate divorce for incompatibility, Blake goes further in demanding the complete freedom of love, regardless of ceremony.

America corresponds to Milton's political works. Both attack their king's policies, and hail the revolution against them; but Blake attempts to achieve the formula of all revolution. *The Marriage of Heaven and Hell* may be compared to *The Christian Doctrine*; but where Milton consolidated the old system, with important alterations, Blake demolished it entirely and proclaimed a totally new view of the universe,—incidentally for the first time overtly attacking Milton's ideas, even suggesting broadly that the Messiah is really the Devil.

In *Europe*, Blake attacked Milton's favorite ideal, Chastity, asserting that it was a product of the Female Will, for which he blamed conventional Christianity, and quoted from the 'Hymn to the Nativity' to date its beginning.

The Four Zoas is an epic with some striking resemblances to *Paradise Lost*, especially in the degeneration of Urizen, whom Blake identifies with Satan.

Milton is a frank attempt to revaluate and correct Milton's chief ideas. The poet enters Blake through his left foot (south—the intellect). Milton's descent from Eternity is a study of the development of his thought, illustrated with quotations from *Paradise Lost*. At the end, Milton sees and renounces his errors.

Jerusalem corresponds to the *History of Britain*, which Blake expands into the fall and resurrection of Albion, the history of all mankind. His daughters are named for the women in that book. Blake's explanation of his free septenaries is a bold expansion of Milton's explanation of his blank verse. In the final apocalypse, Milton appears in the heavens with Chaucer and Shakspere.

Blake also illustrated all Milton's chief poems, except *Samson Agonistes*. No other illustrator was ever so precise in following the text, and no other ever included interpretations of his own.

Thus the works of Milton influenced Blake more than any other book except the Bible. He agreed that Milton was one of the greatest poets, but for better reasons than the world had yet suspected. He knew that Milton had seen clearly and deeply into the mysteries of the human soul, but had not always understood what he saw; that he thought profoundly, but was cramped by traditional theology. Therefore Blake accepted the challenge of Milton's philosophy, and engaged with him in that warfare of ideas which is one of the greatest joys of Eternity, where the soldier fights for truth and calls the enemy his brother.

IV

Notes for a Commentary on Milton

by

Northrop Frye

Victoria College, The University of Toronto (*Canada*)

IV

Notes for a Commentary on Milton

1. *Introduction.*[1]

BLAKE IS A poet of the Bible, and from early life he saw in the Bible the outlines of an epic narrative. This narrative begins with myths of creation, fall, and deluge (which are all the same event in Blake) and goes on to the history of Israel, presented as a sequence of revolutions and captivities. This sequence is interrupted, though not terminated, by the Incarnation, and, after a period of undetermined length, an apocalypse and Last Judgement put an end to history and return us to the world as it was before the Fall. It is natural, then, that Blake's poetic ambitions should have moved steadily in the direction of writing a Christian epic poem that would reshape this narrative and so in its own context justify the ways of God to men—the Miltonic phrase is on the title-page of *Milton*.

Many of Blake's shorter 'prophecies' can be read as episodes from such an epic. *America* and *The Marriage of Heaven and Hell* (1793) deal with the last phase, the French and American

[1] All references to *Milton* are accompanied by the number of the plate, as given in Keynes, *Poetry and Prose of William Blake*, followed after a colon by the number of the line. Of the four copies of *Milton*, the Keynes text adopts the order of the latest and most complete (Copy 'D' in the Keynes-Wolf Census), adding the Preface from the earlier copies. As there is no point in repeating what I have said elsewhere about *Milton*, the reader is respectfully referred, for aspects of the poem not discussed here but falling within my general approach to it, to my *Fearful Symmetry* (Princeton, 1947), especially Chapter Ten.

revolutions being regarded as signs of an imminent apocalypse. *Europe* (1794) begins with the Incarnation, covering the New Testament part of the myth. *The* (*First*) *Book of Urizen* (1794) begins a series of prophetic essays at the other end, of creation and fall. In 1795 came an extraordinary burst of pictorial activity climaxed by over five hundred designs for Young's *Night Thoughts*. In Young's poem, nine 'nights' of vision of which the ninth is a Last Judgement, Blake got a hint for a larger epic scheme of his own. *Vala*, much of which is written on the backs of proofs for the Young designs, has also nine 'nights', the first four dealing with the creation-fall-deluge complex, the next four with four generalized phases of a cycle of history from revolution to decline under tyranny. The last night of this sequence, the eighth, covers, like *Europe*, the period from the Incarnation to Blake's time. The ninth night is an apocalypse, as in Young. This poem was still in manuscript when Blake moved to Felpham and the company of Hayley in 1800, by which time its name had been changed to *The Four Zoas*.

The Four Zoas illustrates a good deal of interest and reading in epic literature. Its original form of a sybil's prophecy shows the influence of the Icelandic Eddas, and possibly of the sixth book of the *Aeneid*, which Blake certainly knew, although he seems more interested in the second: the Laocoon story always fascinated him, and some aspects of his 'Covering Cherub' may be derived from Virgil's Pyrrhus. The names of the first two characters in *The Four Zoas*, Tharmas and Enion, are probably taken from the Thaumas and Eione of Hesiod. Of English epic poets, Blake knew Chaucer and Spenser, and would have found in Chaucer's *House of Fame*, for all its irony, many points of contact with his own Golgonooza. A Chaucerian synonym for fame, *los* or *loos*, may be the source of the name of Blake's great hero.[1]

But Milton, whom he had known and loved from childhood, was always for Blake his primary master both for the Christian epic and for his understanding of the Bible. It was Blake's habit to record his differences rather than his agreements, but even when he is most critical of Milton he shows how closely he is following him. It seems almost incredible, for instance, that the incisive comment on Milton's view of the Trinity in *The Marriage of Heaven and Hell* could have been made by a reader who did not know the *Christian Doctrine*. Besides, in every age Milton has been a political symbol as well as a poet. To the Tory Samuel Johnson Milton was 'an acrimonious and surly republican,' a view which brought a violent reaction from the mildly liberal Cowper. To anyone as far left of centre as Blake, Milton was not only the last of England's major poets, but England's one major prophet as well. Blake's poem, based on his conviction that Milton not only should be 'living at this hour' but actually was, is a vision of Milton as the deliverer of his people, like Milton's own Samson, or, perhaps a closer analogy, as a guardian angel, like Michael in Israel (and, according to *Lycidas*, in England as well). The notion that Blake was primarily concerned to 'correct' Milton's theological and domestic difficulties rests on a story of Crabb Robinson's which is much better ignored.[2]

[1] A volume of Chaucer containing *The House of Fame*, with an illustration engraved by Blake, was published in 1782. I also feel that M. 30:39, 'Ozoth here builds walls of rocks against the surging sea', has some reference to the *Franklin's Tale*.

[2] Blake is alleged to have complained that Milton was grievously in error in saying that the pleasures of sex arose from the Fall. Milton, of course, said nothing of the kind, as Blake, who made at least four illustrations

The immediate effect of Hayley on Blake was to sharpen his sense and increase his knowledge of the epic tradition. Hayley had written a poem about epic poetry, with erudite notes, and even his redoubtable soap opera in heroic couplets, *The Triumphs of Temper*, links itself in a preface with the heroi-comical branch of epic. Besides the usual Classical training of his day (Blake began reading Greek with Hayley), Hayley had a wider knowledge of modern European literatures than was common at that time. Of the few important commissions that Blake got out of Hayley, one of the first was the series of heads of poets, most of them epic poets, done as a frieze for Hayley's library. A man of Blake's intellectual curiosity was unlikely to draw a head of Ercilla without inquiring who Ercilla was, and his education must have rapidly expanded in many directions. Nor was Milton neglected. Hayley, a liberal like Cowper, had written a life of Milton also, and Cowper, when he came to Felpham in 1792, brought with him an unfinished Milton project, of which the central part was his translations of Milton's Latin and Italian poems. This was eventually published by Hayley in 1808, with some assistance from Blake, though both the designing and the engraving commissions were eventually taken away from him.

Blake came to Felpham practically determined to make his stay there a period of definitive vision, and it is not surprising that the immediate result of it should be a poem in the epic tradition with a particular relationship to Milton. Sir Geoffrey Keynes is definite that the '2 Books' of the title-page

of Satan watching the love-play of the unfallen Adam and Eve, knew very well.

originally read '12 Books', and the original *Milton* would undoubtedly have followed the narrative of the scriptural epic as preserved in *The Four Zoas.* After dealing with creation, deluge, the fall of Satan and Adam, and the various phases of the cycle of history, it would have shown the apocalypse consolidating from the wars and tyrannies of the eighteenth century through some crucial act of poetic vision in Blake's own life. The poem referred to in letters to Butts of April and July, 1803, is clearly much longer than the present *Milton,* though there is no evidence that it introduced Milton himself as a character.

When the poem was cut down to two books, only the act of vision remained, and the remainder survives vestigially. The cycle of history is represented by the Bard's Song, which also makes some attempt to work in the Blakean story of the beginning of things. Plate 3, carrying over the account of the creation of the physical world out of Urizen by Los from two earlier prophecies, is a later plate, connected with the Bard's Song by the opening line of Plate 11 (also a later plate), identifying Urizen with the Satan of the Bard's story. The apocalypse appears only in the distance at the end of the poem. Thus the poem as we now have it is, in Milton's language, not a 'diffuse' but a 'brief' epic, not a Blakean *Paradise Lost* but a Blakean *Paradise Regained.* The theme of Blake's poem is a struggle with Satan in which Milton occupies the place that Christ occupies in *Paradise Regained,* and hence it might be described, without a comma, as 'Paradise Regained by John Milton'.

The personal references in Milton are to a time when Blake was getting bored with Felpham and distrustful of Hayley's influence on him—say the earlier months of 1803, before the

Schofield fracas of August. *Milton* as we have it is clearly pre-Schofield in its general setting, though Schofield and his accompanying symbols are mentioned once (M. 21: 59) in an obviously later insertion. The date 1804 on the title-page probably means that by then the writing had been essentially completed and the engraving begun. The serenity of tone makes the end of 1805 practically a *terminus ad quem* for the writing. On December 11 of that year Blake wrote what shows every sign of being intended as the last letter to Hayley. After that came Cromek, the Stothard quarrel, the first Hunt attack, and the 'despair' entry of January 20, 1807. Still later come the bitter epigrams on Hayley, when Blake was recreating in his mind some black thoughts that had passed through it at the time of the Schofield affair. His reference in the 'Public Address' to a poem about his Felpham sojourn which will expose a 'nest of villains' is not to the *Milton* we have, and perhaps indicates that he thought of rewriting it to fit his more neurotic later mood. Fortunately he never did so, and in fact seems to have revised the poem in the same serene spirit in which he wrote it. Plates 3, 4, and 5, which are later, stress the universal rather than the personal aspect of the Satan–Hayley myth with which the poem begins, and the noisy preface disappears from the later copies, in spite of the fact that it contains one of Blake's greatest lyrics. The *engraving* of *Milton* is a by-product of intense concentration on the illustrating of Milton's poems, an activity which extended over a great part of Blake's life, and is remarkably consistent in its iconography. For instance, the 'sixfold emanation' of the poem, illustrated on Plates 19 and 48, reappears as the six spirits surrounding Milton, noted in the description to an illustration to *Il Penseroso* (No. 11), written in 1816.

2. *Structure of the Symbolism: Eden.*

Milton is based on the conception of four levels of vision expounded in a poem written by Blake in the summer of 1801 and sent in a letter to Butts of November 1802. In the highest or Paradisal view of reality (Eden), man is one with God, and everything else is part of a divine, and therefore a human, creation. Imagination attempts to recreate the world in the form in which man originally possessed it. In the next highest view, which is sexual rather than fully human (M. 4 : 5), the view of the lower Paradise or Beulah, the relation of creator and creature becomes the relation of lover and beloved, and the created world becomes an 'emanation' or responsive bride, like Shelley's epipsyche. This view survives in our world as the child's innocent vision, the sense of reality as a protected home. Below this is the world of Generation or experience, which is split into a subjective and an objective aspect. Here the emanation becomes a remote and tantalizing 'female will', and the perceiver is transformed into a 'Spectre' or 'Selfhood', 'a Male Form howling in Jealousy' (M. 3 : 36), who, in the poem 'My Spectre around me', written about the same time as *Milton* and referred to in it (M. 35 : 5), is depicted as tracking through the snow a disappearing mistress who is actually inside him. Below this again is Ulro or hell, the world of 'Single vision & Newton's sleep', divided between an ego and a vast menacing form of 'nature', which to the imagination wavers uncertainly between a paternal and a maternal figure, both equally stupid and cruel.

In ordinary life this hierarchy of worlds is reversed. At the apex of experience is the inscrutable and unthinkably remote world of the stars, the ultimate inspiration for all our belief in fate. Next comes the world we work in, sitting on top of the child's innocent vision, which with the advance of maturity is driven underground into the subconscious. But deeper than the buried child Orc, the terrible boy who bursts out in revolution, there is the buried unfallen humanity Los, the patient smith who forges the golden city (cf. Isa. liv, 16), but who also keeps the world of Generation going as a defence against the ultimate horror of Ulro.

In the 'natural' or common-sense view of reality, as expounded, according to Blake, by Locke, each subject is a separate centre of perception, and each object is a separate thing, things being classified for convenience by their similarities or general resemblances. This process leads from sensation to reflexion, from the concrete to the abstract, 'Within labouring, beholding Without, from Particulars to Generals' (M. 3 : 37). The imaginative view turns the natural one inside out. Here the subject is not at the centre but at the circumference of reality, hence all perceivers are one perceiver, who is the totality of humanity (Albion) and because totally human, divine as well (Jesus). Rilke is close to Blake when he speaks of the poet's perspective as that of an angel containing all time and space, but blind and looking into himself. From this point of view, space is no longer extension (Enitharmon controlled by the fallen Urizen), but form (Enitharmon controlled by Los); time is no longer duration (Spectre of Urthona) but creative life (Los). In Plates 30–31 we learn that the view of space and time as indefinite extensions receding from us is a projection caused by the cramped quarters of our present bodies.

The common-sense view perceives separation and similarity; the imaginative view perceives two kinds of identity. Blake speaks of 'Identities or Things': a thing may be identified *as* itself, yet it cannot be identified except as an individual of a class. The class is its 'living form', not its abstract essence, and form in Blake is a synonym for image, or experienced reality (thus the 'Forms Eternal' of M. 35 : 38 are opposed to what Blake thought of as Platonic forms). All Blake's images and mythical figures are 'minute particulars' or individuals identified with their total forms. Hence they are 'States, Combinations of Individuals' (M. 35 : 10), and can be seen in either singular or collective aspects. Ololon is the sixfold emanation of Milton because Milton had three wives and three daughters, yet also a mighty host descending to the earth and a single virgin in Blake's garden. Blake refers impartially to Ololon as 'she' or 'they'.

Further, all things are identical *with* each other. A man feels identical with himself at the age of seven, although between the man and the child there is little that is similar in regard to form, matter, time, space or personality. And as in the imaginative view all things are within the life of a single eternal and infinite God-Man, all aspects, forms or images of that body are identical. This is a view of things which can only be expressed poetically, through metaphor. The metaphor, in its radical form, is a statement of identification: the hero is a lion; this is that; A is B. When the hero is metaphorically a lion he remains a hero and the lion remains a lion. Hence a world where everything is identical with everything else is not a world of monotonous uniformity, as a world where everything was *like* everything else would be. In the imaginative world everything is one in essence, but infinitely varied in identity, as Blake remarks in a note on Swedenborg. We sometimes use the word identical to mean very similar, as in the phrase 'identical twins', but if twins were really identical they would be the same person, and hence could be different in form, like a tree and a dryad.

The language of religion is instinctively metaphorical: Christ *is* God and Man; in the Trinity three *is* one; the body and blood *are* the bread and wine, and so on. In the Bible, especially in the Book of Revelation, we find a world of total identification, the individual identified with the class, 'all Human Forms identified', as Blake says at the end of his own *Jerusalem*. Hence it is a world in which all things have attained a human instead of a merely natural form. If we ask what the human forms of things are, we have only to look at what man tries to do with them. Man tries to build cities out of stones, and to develop farms and gardens out of plants; hence the city and garden are the human forms of the mineral and vegetable worlds respectively. In the apocalypse, then, all aspects of reality are seen in their human forms; each individual is identical with its class or living form, and all living forms are identical with, and therefore eternally different from, one another. To illustrate in a table:

1. The *divine* world is a world in which all 'gods', or aspects of infinite and eternal humanity, are One God. There are four such aspects in Blake, the four 'Zoas' or living creatures who in Ezekiel's vision make up the spiritual body of the Word. Some knowledge of them is assumed by Blake, and for reasons of space has to be assumed here also. Albion fell, like Milton's Adam, through idolatrous adoration of his female principle, though, unlike Adam, he could create her out of his own body. The result was that Luvah or Orc, the sexual (ὄρχις) aspect of him, assumed control in place of the intellectual one (M. 21 : 21; M. 38 : 39), and plunged us all into a world domi-

nated by a sense of sexual shame (represented by the accusing eagle who watches the sleeping Albion on Plate 42).

2. The *spiritual* or angelic world is a world in which all spirits or angels are One Spirit. The fact that this world is out of physical reach is expressed by associating it with fire, in which fallen man cannot live, and with the heavenly bodies. Angels have traditionally been the spirits of sun, moon and stars; the imagination, as Blake says in a famous passage in the Rossetti MS, sees the sun as a company of angels, and the One Spirit descends to man as a single, though infinitely varied, tongue of flame. In Blake there are seven of these 'angels of the divine presence' or 'Eyes of God', and they appear in human history as seven progressive conceptions of God, ending with Jesus. They are listed on Plate 14 and instruct Milton in the doctrine of identity on Plate 35. The second coming of Jesus, which ends history, introduces an eighth (Albion or redeemed man): hence Ololon, the heroine of *Milton* whose appearance prefigures the apocalypse, is associated with a 'Starry Eight'.

3. The *human* world is a world in which all men are One Man, or expressed in terms of sexual rather than social love, a world in which a Bridegroom and a Bride are one flesh. This human world extends over the whole of what we ordinarily think of as non-human nature (M. 27 : 41), for, as the universe is a divine creation, it is also a human creation when God and Man are one.

4. The *animal* world is a world of domesticated animals, of which the sheep has a conventional priority in the Bible, for a world in which the lion lies down with the lamb is clearly conceived from the lamb's point of view. Hence the imaginative or human animal world is a world in which all animals are a single sheepfold, and all sheep One Lamb.

5. The *vegetable* world is a world in which all plants are a garden or farm, the Eden and Promised Land of the Bible. All trees in the garden are One Tree of Life; all plants on the farm are a single harvest and vintage, the bread and wine of which are identical with the body and blood of the One Lamb of the animal world.

6. The *mineral* world is a city of streets and highways, a city in which all buildings are One Temple, a house of many mansions, and that temple One (precious) Stone, the corner stone of Zion.

7. The *chaotic* world, represented by the sea, disappears in the apocalypse (Rev. xxi, 1), its place being taken by a circulating river of fresh water ('the deeps shrink to their fountains', as Blake says in *America*). This river is the water of life restored to man, and as it is identical with the circulating blood of man's risen body all water is a single 'Globule of Blood', as Blake calls it.

In Blake, as in the Bible, Jesus is the unifying principle which identifies all these images with one another. Jesus *is* God and Man; he *is* the bread and wine, the body and blood, the tree, bread and water of life, the vine of which we are branches, the corner stone of the city, and his body *is* the temple. In the apocalypse the Globule of Blood is the sun (M. 31 : 23), for sun, moon and stars are inside the risen body of Christ, and are hence identical with the gold and gems of which the City of God is composed. Further, as risen man can live in fire, all the above images may be thought of as burning: the tree is a burning tree, like a candlestick or the bush of the Exodus; the stones burn with a gem-like flame, and the Jehovah of the Bible is 'no other than he who dwells in flaming fire'. A note scribbled on the back of a sketch for the last plate of *Milton* speaks of returning 'from flames of fire tried & pure & white'. The poet who sees the world in a grain of sand and heaven in a wild flower, and who identifies earth and heaven in vision, has the same conception of identity as that of the famous Buddhist prayer to the jewel in the lotus.

Two other identifications are of importance. In the opening stanza of the 'Introduction' to the *Songs of Experience*, we are told a good deal about Blake's view of the poet. The poet is one 'Who Present, Past, & Future, sees': in vision all times are one. But if all times are one, all spaces are one too: if all time is an eternal present, all space is an infinite presence. The poet is of the tradition of the Hebrew prophets deriving from the Word of God that walked in the garden of Eden and discovered the fall of man; yet he also calls himself, as he does in *Milton*, a 'Bard,' a word with its roots in the British tradition. The imaginative form of Israel, the Garden of Eden or Promised Land, is the same place as the imaginative form of Britain, usually called Atlantis, and the famous hymn 'And did those feet in ancient time', which begins *Milton*, identifies the two.

In the ritual of the Eucharist man eats the bread and wine which 'is' the body and blood of a God-Man. The ritual dramatizes the Fall: the true sacrament for Blake is the formation of a true human society, which is an apocalyptic process separating the individual from the ego or Selfhood, clod-love from pebble-love. This apocalyptic sacrament is to be conceived more as God eating man than as man eating God: a 'harvest and vintage' in which the imaginative form of man is identified with all other forms, and the chaff and lees of the Selfhood are thrown away. The wars of Blake's time are interpreted as the treading of an apocalyptic winepress, following

Isaiah; the growth of science (M. 27 : 18) as the gathering of an apocalyptic harvest. In the earlier *Europe* these signs are the French Revolution and Newton respectively. At the beginning of the poem, on Plate 2, we see wheat and grapes lit up by a huge star or comet representing the descent of Milton; at the end, on Plate 50, the naked female figure in the centre appears to represent the identification of vegetable and human forms.

3. *Structure of the Symbolism: Ulro.*

This world of total and realized metaphor is heaven: its opposite is hell, the pure state of nature of which Blake took so low a view. Ulro is the world as it would appear to humanity at the beginning of the Fall, without a single image of human desire, or form of human work, yet established in it—no habitations, no cultivation, nothing but suggestions of indifference, mystery, inscrutable fate, a relentless fight to survive, and loneliness. The demonic vision of reality is an elaborate parody of the apocalyptic vision. Error disappears only when recognized as error, and error can be recognized only as the opposite of truth. Blake came increasingly to think of the apocalypse in negative terms as a growing consolidation of the natural vision. Hence the central figure of the demonic outlook, Satan, is the youngest son of Los, brought forth 'Refusing Form in vain' (M. 3 : 41) and 'permitted to imitate' (M. 44 : 25) the unfallen state. Here is the form of the demonic imitation:

1. The *divine* world begins in the perception of a non-human power and will in nature, 'The Fairies, Nymphs, Gnomes, & Genii of the Four Elements' (M. 34 : 20). These spirits, with

the advance of natural science, move further away, chiefly into the stars, and become gods. Such gods are conceived, on the analogy of the demonic human society, as inscrutable tyrants, jealous of their privileges, and while they do not exist, the results of believing in them do. One of them is usually in supreme control, asserting that he is 'God alone' and that 'There is no other' (M. 9 : 26). In the demonic vision everything is hierarchic, leading up to an ego at the top, in contrast to the Christ who is a total form, and so self-evidently one. This solitary super-ego, or old man of the sky, Newton's Pantocrator (M. 4 : 11), Blake calls 'Nobodaddy' in the Rossetti MS, 'Urizen' (fallen) in the earlier prophecies, and 'Satan' in *Milton* and *Jerusalem*. The essential attribute of Blake's Satan is death, and he works within man as what we should now call the death-impulse, the inner traitor of the soul who, like Judas Iscariot, eventually goes to his own place (M. 11 : 12; cf. M. 28 : 41).

2. The *spiritual* world is a society of self-righteous demons, who take possession of man to destroy him. They originate of course from the star-gods of a fatalistic view of divinity, and are usually represented in *Jerusalem* by the twelve sons of Albion, the number being zodiacal. As the true spirits are all One Spirit or tongue of flame, so evil spirits are all one 'False Tongue', or Satan as accuser of sin (M. 2 : 10; cf. James iii, 6). This false tongue is called by Blake the 'Covering Cherub', who is to Satan what the Holy Spirit is to Jesus. The Covering Cherub is the serpent of Eden who is identified with the visionary Prince of Tyre, the archetypal tyrant, in Ezekiel xxviii, a chapter which underlies Blake's description of the fall of Satan in Plate 9.

3. The *human* world is a society of tyrants and victims, with a

supreme tyrant usually in control. Such societies in the Bible are typified by Egypt and Babylon, and the tyrants by Pharaoh and Nebuchadnezzar. The individual in such a society is a Selfhood who creates the cruel and lazy sky-gods in his own image. Corresponding to the Bride, the demonic vision has a harlot, the Whore of Babylon whose name is Mystery, the opposite of revelation or apocalypse.

4. The *animal* world is a society of tyrants and victims also, and its symbols in Blake are either beasts of prey or parasites, many of them listed on Plate 29. 'Everything has its Vermin,' Blake says, and among the beasts of prey are the serpent of Eden and the two monsters who appear at the end of Job, behemoth and leviathan. These are associated by Blake with the military and naval warfare of his own time, and in his 1809 Exhibition he saw them in charge of Pitt and Nelson respectively. In the Bible leviathan is identified with Pharaoh (Ezek. xxix, 3), and Nebuchadnezzar turns into a variety of behemoth.

5. The *vegetable* world is a heath, forest or wilderness, called Entuthon Benython (the second part of which may be connected with the Greek *βένθος*, depth). Its individual form is the Tree of Mystery, the self-enrooting banyan of 'The Human Abstract', which is also the oak worshipped by the Druids, and, in the Bible, the tree of moral knowledge, the Cross and the barren fig-tree.

6. The *mineral* world, or demonic city, is featured by hierarchically-shaped buildings like the pyramid or tower of Babel, servile architecture as Ruskin would call them, and by structures which, like the furnace, the winepress and the mill, imprison fire or disintegrate form (M. 43 : 16 ff.).

7. The *chaotic* world is the sea (or snow or desert), the sea which as the 'Red' Sea recalls the spilt blood of fallen man (M.

31 : 63). As the Dead Sea or salt lake it is called Udan Adan (M. 25 : 60), and as the Atlantic Ocean it is the 'Sea of Time and Space' which separates England and America and conceals the Atlantis which is the imaginative form of both.

All demonic images may be also identified with one another, in fact must be if *Milton* is to be read with any comprehension. The entire universe of nature is the 'dark Satanic mills' of a cyclical labyrinth (M. 14 : 43), and this universe is, in relation to the real world, both underground and (adopting the deluge version of the Fall) under water. It is an embryonic world, described by Blake as the Mundane Shell (M. 19 : 21 ff.), and within it is the vast inter-related mass of spawning generative life which Blake calls the 'Polypus' and identifies with Orc or Luvah, the natural body of which we are members (M. 31 : 31; M. 38 : 24). The Covering Cherub may be seen in the stars who mark the circumference of the single vision, for Satan is above all a sky-god or lord of the natural heaven, a dragon whose tail drew down a third of the stars (M. 13 : 26). As his journey in *Paradise Lost* shows, his empire extends over both chaos and what we call the cosmos. As leviathan, Satan is not only a sea-monster but the sea itself, the sea that covers Atlantis, Sodom, Pharaoh's Egyptians, and, according to Milton, the Garden of Eden after the flood. To find Atlantis again we have only to drain the sea, not the Atlantic Ocean, but the 'Sea of Time and Space' on top of our imaginations (M. 17 : 36 ff.).

Another feature of the Ulro vision requiring comment is the 'female will', the separated objective world that confronts us in the fallen perspective. The outer world of nature is a 'Female Space' (M. 11 : 6) because, like a 'harlot coy' increasing her price by pretending to be a virgin, it continually retreats from the perceiver. The perceiver is a human being, who may be a man or a woman—in other words Blake's 'female will' has nothing to do with human women except when women dramatize it in their sexual rituals, as they do, for instance, in the Courtly Love convention. The relation of humanity to external nature is shown as a cycle of four phases in *The Mental Traveller*, a poem dating from the Felpham period, where nature is a female figure appearing first as a mother to an infant, then as a wife to an adult, then as a daughter to an old man, and then as a mirage to a ghost. None of these relations is quite true: the mother is actually an old nurse, the wife a temporary mistress, the daughter a changeling, and the mirage an outward reflexion of the 'emanation', which is inside the mind. Thus in every phase nature is both virgin and harlot, unpossessed and mocking. In the first phase her Blakean name is Tirzah, in the second Vala, in the third Rahab, in the fourth the Shadowy Female. All four names are important in *Milton*. The Shadowy Female is associated with the Lilith of Isaiah in M. 20 : 43. Rahab is identified with Egypt and leviathan in the Bible, and by Blake with the apocalyptic Whore (M. 46 : 22). Tirzah in the Exodus story is one of five sisters, daughters of Zelopehad (M. 31 : 58), who demand a separate female inheritance: these five are the five fallen senses in Blake, the five foolish virgins without light. Their names are given in M. 19 : 11 and elsewhere.

'Natural religion' is called an 'impossible absurdity' (M. 46 : 13), but it is not a mere intellectual error: it is rather the working of the death-wish in human life. All human work, art and prophecy go to build up the city and garden of a free, happy and equal human civilization, but all such work implies the predominance of a human over a subhuman vision of life.

Natural religion operates in three stages: natural law, the admiration for the automatism of external nature; moral law, the attempt to imitate this automatism in human life, and finally 'accusation of sin', or attempts to enforce conformity as a supreme virtue. At each state the underlying form of natural religion, a deep distrust in the worth of human life itself, becomes more clearly revealed. Human sacrifice is the purest form of this, but war and slavery are also products of shame, the contempt for life that springs from the thwarting of the sexual drive. For war is always treated by Blake, with a psychological insight which would be startling to those who do not know him, as a sexual perversion, ending in 'Glory & Victory a Phallic Whip'.[1] This is how war is visualized in Plate 29.

As for Blake's condemnation of Newton, even that shows how deeply Miltonic a poet Blake was. In *Paradise Lost* Raphael refuses to answer Adam's questions about cosmology: he does not mean that Adam's descendants should not study astronomy, but that in preparing for a crucial ordeal in his own life Adam should be concentrating on the Word of God within him and not on the works of God without. Blake's view of Newtonian science is similar: it is not its truth but the mental attitude to it that is in question. If the beauty of nature's mathematical order can encourage men to think that the miseries they perpetrate in their own society are inevitable or of little importance, its study can be a pernicious narcotic. We tend to think of the eighteenth century rather sentimentally as an age of common sense and enlightenment: Blake thought of it as an age of imperialistic war and slavery which finally erupted in the senseless hysteria of the Napoleonic wars and in

[1] David V. Erdman: *Blake: Prophet Against Empire* (Princeton, 1954), 387.

the ruthless extermination of culture 'Where Human Thought is crush'd beneath the iron hand of Power' (M. 27 : 5).

4. *Structure of the Symbolism: Generation.*

The world that we ordinarily live in is not heaven, but neither is it quite hell. It is the world of experience, a world not under the wrath but under the law. Heaven and hell, Eden and Ulro, form a great antithesis of eternal life and eternal death, and the whole effort of imagination and art is directed toward separating them. The rhythm of existence in this world, where the presiding genius is Orc or Luvah, Blake's Eros, is cyclical, following the movements of the heavenly bodies. History shows a series of cycles: seven major ones, or 'Eyes of God', since the beginning of time, and twenty-seven minor ones, or 'Churches', from Adam's time to our own. Each major cycle begins with a revolt against tyranny, and gradually ages into a new tyranny as the pressure of natural religion gets stronger.

First of all, in Blake's version of history, were the Druids, the survivors of Atlantis, who developed a culture of megalithic temples, tree and serpent worship, and finally expired in a frenzy of human sacrifice, burning victims in wicker cages (M. 41 : 11). Druid architecture is illustrated in the early part of the poem, in Plates 4 and 6. The Druids were giants, but their culture established the pattern followed after men collapsed into their present human forms. They belonged to the second 'Eye' of Moloch; with the third, Elohim, human life began as we know it. Adam represents the 'limit of contraction' (M. 14 : 21), or the nadir of the fall of man's body, hence nature, the objective counterpart of that body, 'is a

Vision of the Science of the Elohim' (M. 31 : 65). The story of Adam is also associated with trees and serpents. The sixth 'Eye', Jehovah, was Hebrew civilization, which went through the four stages summarized in *The Four Zoas*, of revolt (birth of Orc), study of natural law (Urizen exploring his dens), moral law (crucifixion of Orc) and a final blood-bath of mass murder. This last stage is symbolized by a flood, out of which an 'ark', or historical womb, preserves the embryo of new life.[1]

The Exodus story tells how a revolt against Egyptian tyranny was gradually 'perverted to ten commands', as Blake says in *America*. The Israelites were trying to reach a new Jerusalem and a Promised Land identical with the Garden of Eden. The Exodus story says that Moses, the spirit of the law, died at the boundary of the Promised Land, the conquest of which was achieved by Joshua, who has the same name as Jesus. Symbolically, this means that the Israelites never really came out of the wilderness, and the reign of the law did not end, nor was the conquest of the genuine Promised Land begun, until Jesus was given Joshua's name. The four stages of Israelite culture were, first, the revolt against Egypt; second, the wandering in the labyrinthine wilderness; third, the giving of the moral law and the crucifixion of Orc as the brazen serpent on the pole, and finally an entry into 'Canaan' accompanied by annihilation wars.

The career of Jesus corresponds closely to the Exodus: he is

[1] Hence Satan, at the crisis of *Milton*, appears as a sea-monster or leviathan (M. 43: 9 ff.), and Ololon as a 'Moony Ark' (M. 49: 7). For the iconography of the 'moony ark' in Blake, see Keynes, *Blake Studies* (1949), 42, and Ruthven Todd, *Tracks in the Snow* (1946), 37. Similarly the 'female will' aspect of Ololon disappears like the dove (M. 49: 6; Gen. viii, 12).

led into Egypt, wanders in the desert, preaches the gospel from a mountain, gathers twelve followers, is crucified like the brazen serpent, and conquers the true Promised Land. But the cycle of civilization he started, the seventh 'Eye', symbolized in Blake by Lazarus (M. 26 : 26) and by Theotormon (M. 24 : 38), also had its core of natural religion, inherited partly from Jewish and partly from Classical culture. The progress of the Christian cycle is traced in *Europe*, which begins with an echo of the *Nativity Ode* (echoed again in *Milton* when the great 'Vision of beatitude' begins, M. 27 : 71). The *Nativity Ode*, like most of Milton's earlier poems, has two levels of nature. One is the fallen or corrupt nature trying to 'hide her guilty front with innocent snow', Blake's Leutha; the other is a divinely sanctioned order symbolized by the harmony of the spheres. It is part of the argument of *Europe* (and of *Milton*) that this divinely sanctioned order is in fact the very world of the false gods that Jesus came to drive away. By Newton's time it has disappeared entirely into an invisible world of 'primary qualities', and the period after Newton begins its death-agonies as a new cycle rises in America.

The world of Generation has a structure of symbolism parallel to Eden and Ulro, most of the symbols being derived from the Exodus narrative. Thus:

1. The *divine* world is a world of moral gods, like the jealous Jehovah of the ten commandments. Such gods are stupid and priggish, caring nothing about art or imagination but only about the proper ritual for themselves and for a morality of mediocrity, but they are not actively vicious unless cornered or threatened. The helpless *dieu fainéant* who appears in the early Job plates, unable to prevent Satan doing as he likes,

represents this aspect of Jehovah, whose destruction by Milton is depicted in Plate 18.

2. The *spiritual* (always in Blake a synonym of mental or intellectual) world is a world of generalizations or abstract ideas, hazy reflexions derived as a residue from sense experience, which are called, like the individual who holds them, 'spectres'. They originate in natural law, and they develop moralism because they are conceived in panic (we speak of grasping or seizing such ideas) and express themselves in aggression. Precepts and arguments, unlike the concrete examples of art and experience, can be used only as weapons: they must refute or be refuted, and hence, as described on Plate 30, they are either cowards or bullies until liberalized by being made into the images of art.

3. The *human* world is a society of the respectable people of the law and the sub-respectable, the latter including both geniuses and criminals, for morality cannot distinguish 'tygers of wrath' from ordinary beasts of prey. In a true human society all men are brothers, and the parental relation is subordinated to the fraternal one. In Generation the chief symbols of society are parental, implying that as many as possible are to be kept in leading strings. In Blake the 'priest' is sinister and the 'monk' benevolent because the former is called father and the latter brother, and religion dominated by father and mother symbols is a religion that has fallen under the law.

4. The animal world, not important in *Milton*, is the exact counterpart of the human one, a society of respectable animal slaves, 'horses of instruction' or sheep designed to be fleeced, along with outlaws like the tiger and the wolf.

5. The *garden* of the ordinary world is symbolized by Blake as 'Canaan', i.e., the land possessed by a people who have given

up the real Promised Land and settled down under the Mosaic law and the Levitical priesthood. Canaan of course includes eighteenth-century Europe, its counterpart in the next cycle. Israel has twelve tribes because society's pattern is that of the zodiacal cycle of nature, and the forty-eight cities assigned to the Levites (Joshua xxi, 41; M. 43 : 1) correspond to the remaining constellations (M. 41 : 54). We are told that the Israelites were frightened away from the Promised Land by 'giants' or 'ghosts' ('Rephaim', M. 31 : 57), and hence in Canaan would be still under the domain of the same giants, who are actually the constellations marking the limits of the gigantic world perceived by the dwarfed eye, which 'shrinks the Organs of Life till they become Finite & itself seems Infinite' (M. 11 : 6). Of these giants, who in the aggregate make up the Covering Cherub, the most important are Og, Sihon, and Anak. They are politically the tyrants of Canaan, such as William Pitt and Napoleon, intellectually the ideas derived from a world under the stars (M. 41 : 50), and psychologically the moral censors who keep us from using our imaginations (M. 22 : 35).

6. The *city* of the world of experience is the earthly Jerusalem, with the temple at the centre. The shape of this temple —an outer court for Gentiles, an inner court for the people of the law, and an inmost Holy of Holies with nothing there, suggests the hierarchic structure of a moral society and the structure of the generalizing mind, which moves from sensation to reflexion to unreality. The symbolism of Jewish ritual has been traditionally regarded by Christians as a concealed allegory of what is revealed in the New Testament, and for Blake the Book of Revelation in particular is an imaginative translation of the Book of Exodus. Aaron's breastplate has

twelve precious stones symbolizing the remoteness of Israel from the zodiac;[1] the City of God has twelve precious stones identifying the stars with the body of risen man. The lament of the Shadowy Female on Plate 20 contains several allusions to Aaron's costume, and illustrates once more the fact that priests always worship a female will. That is why both the ark with its curtains and the temple with its veil over a 'secret place' (destroyed by Jesus) bear a marked resemblance to the female genitalia (cf. M. 41 : 40; M. 43 : 25 f.).

7. The *watery* world includes, first, the Jordan, and second, the four fallen rivers of Eden. Three of these, the Nile, Euphrates and Tigris, are now the rivers of Egypt, Babylon, and Assyria: the fourth is identified with the Arnon, which flows westward into the Dead Sea. The Arnon marked the boundary of the empire of Moloch (*P. L.* i, 399), to whom parents sacrificed their children. Hence the Arnon symbolizes what Blake calls 'Storgous Appetite' (cf. M. 38 : 30), or the process of ensuring that the next generation will be exactly like its predecessor. The significance of the Jordan and the Arnon will become clearer later.

Christianity has always seen in the law an aspect that is fulfilled by the gospel, and another aspect that is annihilated by it. For Blake this means that Generation is the battlefield of the imaginative and natural visions, and that there is a dialectic

[1] 'Plac'd in the order of the stars', *Europe* 12; cf. Josephus, *Antiq.* iii, 7. An edition of Josephus, published in 1786, has illustrations engraved by Blake. The Classical tradition, attacked in the Preface to *Milton*, is thought of by Blake as much the same structure of natural religion as the Jewish priesthood, which is what Blake means by his Laocoon aphorism: 'What we call Antique Gems are the Gems of Aaron's Breast Plate.' The breastplate is also associated with the Covering Cherub (M. 9:31 f.).

forming within the natural cycle, which eventually will separate Eden from Ulro and stop the cycle from turning. On one side are the world's unacknowledged legislators, the artists and prophets, generally ridiculed or persecuted in their time, and hence called by Blake the 'Reprobate'. They do not form a social class, for 'Every honest man is a Prophet', and every Christian is an artist; but genius and sanctity are at their centre. On the other side are the 'Elect', the rulers and teachers (kings and priests) who support the natural or demonic vision. Everything in their world that makes it better than a hell on earth (Ulro) has been the work of previous artists and prophets: the Elect do not improve anything, but are 'Created continually' (M. 5 : 11) by the perpetual-motion machine of ritual and morality. Between them come the great mass of humanity, who are victims of tyranny yet civilized by the imagination, and whom Blake calls the 'Redeemed'.

Reprobate and Redeemed form imaginative contraries in this world, and as 'Without Contraries is no progression', the dialectic of their 'Mental Fight' gradually pulls the honest and well-meaning away from superstition towards vision, the ultimate goal being expressed by the verse 'Would to God that all the Lord's people were Prophets,' which Blake adopts as the motto of *Milton*, probably because Milton had used it in an unusually apocalyptic passage in *Areopagitica*. The Elect are something to be separated from, not something to be fought with: they represent a 'Negation', not a contrary (M. 33, design), and when the struggle is complete the Negation disappears (M. 46 : 32 ff.). They cannot be fought with because they cannot understand a conflict of 'States', but only a conflict of individuals (M. 35 : 22), based on the illusory contraries of moral good and evil. In Satan's world, 'where the

Contraries of Beulah War beneath Negation's Banner' (M. 38 : 23) we have the parody-conflicts of war and hunting as we know them (M. 39 : 2 f.), where we pretend that we are good and the enemy bad.

5. *Structure of the Symbolism: Beulah.*

The child lives in the state of innocence, not because he is morally good, but because he accepts the world as his home, and assumes that friendly animals, benevolent guardians, a green and pleasant land and a life of spontaneous enjoyment are his birthright. He then grows up into the less intelligible world of experience, and the innocent vision is driven into the subconscious, to become a perversion of sexual energy. Here we have the world gingerly explored by modern psychology, the furnace of frustrated desire underneath consciousness, the human volcano with the bound Orc, that will some day, Blake prophesies, explode and burn up the sky-world of experience sitting on top of it. Hence Beulah, for all its association with 'the weak & weary' (M. 34 : 1) is also a potentially destructive force. We read of 'the wind of Beulah that unroots the rocks & hills' (M. 7 : 33), and it is the source of the terror as well as the beauty of art, the inspiration of which comes from Beulah (M. 2 : 1).

But an explosion by itself will do nothing: human desire must fulfil itself as an achieved vision. Blake's conception of vision includes *telos*: the oak tree is the unconscious vision of the acorn; the eternal city and garden are the conscious vision of man, the reason or bounding outline of his desire. Although Orc appears to be smothered under the world of Urizen, the real power that keeps him chained is Los, who has the task of articulating human vision, and so of restoring the golden age, as Blake says of his own art. Such an achieved vision, the total form of art, prophecy and imagination in this world, is the central aspect of Blake's Beulah, which has also a symbolic structure parallel to the others:

1. The *divine* world is the world of Los, the spirit of art and prophecy, the power working in man to create the human form of the world. He is also time, a mental category which we may perceive in either of two ways. In the natural vision time continually falls away from a beginning, and in this vision everything seems to be lost and to disappear in time. In the imaginative vision time continually moves forward to an end or final cause, and in this vision everything is preserved, until time becomes timeless (M. 24 : 18 ff.).

2. The *spiritual* or mental world is the world of Enitharmon or space, in its imaginative sense of form, in contrast to the fallen sense of extension given in *Europe*. Blake calls it Cathedron, and it is a world where in mental life the truculent and panic-stricken spectres of polemic are brought out of the dark cave of 'speculation' into the realized imagery of art, and where in physical life the powers of a non-human nature, the spirits of the elements, become living forms or 'woven bodies'.

3. The *human* world is the world of the sons of Los, who are not the spirits of the arts so much as the imaginative attitudes which produce all genuine work (cf. M. 30 : 14). Of the sons of Los, seven are particularly mentioned in *Milton*: five of them appeared in *Europe* in their perverted forms.[1]

[1] Sotha, who has African connexions, probably comes from Sothis, the Egyptian name for Sirius, the basis of Egyptian chronology. Ozoth appears to be derived from azoth, the alchemical panacea of Paracelsus. The sevens

4, 5, 6. The *animal* and *vegetable* worlds constitute the 'Cultivated land' (M. 29 : 42) of true work, or imaginative commerce, which Blake calls Allamanda, and the *city* of the imagination is the palace of art, or Golgonooza, the central gate of which is called Luban.

7. The world of experience is 'under' the law: moral virtue and the predictability of nature are its ceiling, the 'vault of paved heaven', as it appears to the lunatic of the 'Mad Song'. But the top of the moral world is the bottom of the imagination. Morality and science are the minimum basis of the imaginative life, or what is called in the 'Introduction' to the *Songs of Experience* its 'starry floor'. The genuine science of law that works in the basement of the imagination is called Bowlahoola. *Milton* is pervaded by Blake's later feeling that the fallen world is providentially protected by Los as a defence against chaos or non-existence, symbolized by the sea (M. 43 : 14; hence Bowlahoola is founded by Tharmas the sea-god as his own boundary, M. 26 : 48). The building of the Mundane Shell and 'Mathematic power,' associated with Urizen in *The Four Zoas*, are transferred to Los in *Milton* (M. 38 : 31; M. 31 : 38), though the emphasis is thrown on the 'continual' building of a barrier which, as Blake says elsewhere, is burned up as soon as men cease to behold it (cf. M. 29 : 60).

---

and eights of M. 30 are connected with the fact that the 'Eyes of God' appear either as seven or as eight (see above, and cf. M. 17:5 f.). For this curious ambiguity between seven and eight, which runs all through the history of symbolism, see C. G. Jung, *Psychology and Alchemy* (1953), 66. Of other numbers in Blake, the number of consolidated error is usually one short of the imaginative number. Thus the awakened Albion has fifty-two counties and twenty-eight cities, hence error has fifty-one gods (M. 41:18) and twenty-seven churches (M. 41:35).

In Beulah the amorphous society of man begins to assume the shape of the single human body of the awakened Albion, hence these last three worlds, commerce, art and law, may be seen as the emerging forms of the circulatory, cerebral, and unconscious digestive systems of an infinite Man. Correspondingly, nature begins to take on its proper form of a female 'emanation', a form loved because created. Christianity preserves this symbolism when it speaks of the Church as the Bride of Christ; but in Blake the creature in eternity is female and the creator male, and human beings are not creatures in the resurrection. In the imaginative view Enitharmon with her 'looms' that weave bodies is a benevolent mother, not a vacuous 'fate'; the city of Jerusalem becomes a bride; the sun and moon appear as the emanations, Ocalythron and Elynittria, of the spirits of prophecy and art, Rintrah and Palamabron. The garden becomes the fruitful land, the black but comely bride of the Song of Songs, the liberated Earth of the first two poems in the *Songs of Experience*, the land which is 'married' (the meaning of the word Beulah; see Isa. lxii, 4). The river becomes the genuine 'milky way' (M. 39 : 50 ff.), the nourishing stream which, in the form of Ololon (M. 23 : 15), is the heroine of *Milton*.[1]

[1] Other forms of the black but comely female in Blake are Oothoon, the heroine of *Visions of the Daughters of Albion*, and the Lyca of 'The Little Girl Lost'. Lyca, like the little black boy, comes from the southern clime, and Oothoon, like the chimney sweep, is black in captivity and white in the imaginative world. Oothoon makes her appearance just at the end of the poem, on Plate 49, as one of the dark clouds of Los bearing the fertilizing rain. See Erdman, *op. cit.*, 221, 367. Erdman sees in the sequence of place names at the end of Plate 49 a parable of the Blakes returning from Felpham to London. Elynittria seems to be developed anagrammatically from artillery, in its original sense of a shower of arrows (cf. lines 2 and 43 of M. 5). 'Arrows of desire' are appropriate to a Blakean Diana or moon-goddess. Ocalythron, goddess of the sun, may conceivably be from ὄ κᾶλος θρόνος.

A human being 'has no Body distinct from his Soul': he has either a spiritual body or a natural body, depending on which world he lives in. The things he creates are 'souls' to which he gives bodily form (M. 28 : 13 ff.). Beulah, Blake's Gardens of Adonis, is the place from which 'souls' come and to which they return, and as described here (Plates 33–34) and in *The Book of Thel*, most of its inhabitants are wistful and timid desires seeking embodiment. It is not a place where 'Mental Fight' can be carried on (M. 33 : 3), but a resting place after the results of the fight have been achieved. We need this point to understand Blake's treatment of its predominant moods of pity and love.

6. *Conclusion: Structure of the Narrative.*

At this point a full commentary on *Milton* could begin: here we must be content with summary. After Preface and Invocation, we have first a 'Bard's Song', the theme of which is the cyclical movement of an 'Eye' of history from revolt to collapse, an expanded form of the version given in the Argument to *The Marriage of Heaven and Hell*. Rintrah in Blake is the spirit of prophecy who has the 'Science of Wrath': that is, he is the spirit in man capable of complete imaginative detachment from worldliness. Wrath is the disinterested and impersonal vision of life contemplating death, and is the opposite of anger or irritation. Rintrah is the spirit of Elijah and John the Baptist, the fiery prophet of the desert, and in art he survives as the spirit of the sublime, the vision of a Milton or a Michelangelo which is as far away as art can get from the mundane. Palamabron is the more delicate and refined spirit of the beautiful which appears in high civilizations. Rintrah is the imaginative pioneer breaking the Mundane Shell with the 'plough': Palamabron follows cultivating it with the 'harrow'. In this world all such effort is temporary, and sooner or later Satan, the dusty 'Miller of Eternity', appears, like the button-moulder of *Peer Gynt*, to grind everything down again.

Palamabron, unlike Rintrah, is in the world: he has the 'Science of Pity', and is so close to the world that sooner or later Satan begins producing imitations of him, or vice versa. When this happens, culture becomes decadent or barbaric, and the cycle must begin over again in the prophetic wrath of Rintrah. Rintrah as Elijah was reborn once as John the Baptist, and it is time for him to be reborn again. The crucial phase of the cycle is always the collision between Palamabron and Satan, when Palamabron must remember that he is Rintrah's brother, with the same power of detaching himself wholly from the world, and not Satan's brother, regardless of his sympathy for Satan's victims. Blake himself experienced such a collision at Felpham, where the role of Palamabron was played by himself, that of Satan by Hayley, and that of Rintrah by Blake's real brother Robert, dead but still alive.[1]

Rintrah and Palamabron are the two 'Witnesses' of Rev. xi (M. 24 : 59 refers to Rev. xi, 8), who are Moses and Elijah, the

[1] The association of Robert with Rintrah is made clear by Plate 37, where the iconography is that of pure imagination (star entering *right* foot, *four* stone steps behind). For the significance of Satan's going over to Rintrah, a Saul among the prophets (M. 9:12), see *Fearful Symmetry*, 329. Blake's early letters from Felpham twice speak of Hayley as a brother. The conception of two brothers, one dead and one a murderer of the imagination, suggests Cain and Abel, who illustrate the conclusion of the Bard's Song at the top of Plate 15. For the origin of the 'plough' and 'harrow' symbols in Blake's mind, see the letter to Butts of Sept. 23, 1800. Incidentally, if the plates of the Bard's Song are read in the order of the 'C' copy (2, 7, 4, 6, 3, 8 ff., omitting 5), the narrative will be easier to follow.

law and the prophets, Rintrah being the 'Reprobate' Elijah figure. The two aspects of annihilation and fulfilment in the conception of Moses or the law are symbolized by the story of the struggle of Michael and Satan over the body of Moses, which Blake adapts for *Milton*. Satan is, of course, 'Elect' and Palamabron, separated from Satan and joined to Rintrah, is of the 'Redeemed' class. As Blake is Palamabron, this means that Blake is redeemed by the return of Milton. The conception of three classes seems to have come from the 'Goon' of the *Bhagavadgita*, as they are called in the Wilkins translation Blake read. Blake returns to them in the *Descriptive Catalogue*, where he speaks of a strong or sublime man, a man of beauty or pathos, and an ugly man who represents both 'the human reason' and 'the incapability of intellect'—a typically Blakean equation. According to the newly discovered inscription on the gate in the frontispiece to *Jerusalem*, the Druidic trilithon represents a geometrical or abstract form of the perversion of the relations of the three classes, the 'Sublime & Pathos' being the uprights and the fallen reason covering them.

The Bard's Song concludes with the lament of Leutha, who is the emanation or imaginative world of Satan. Thus she is the hell he lives in, and, as a deliberate echo from *Paradise Lost* informs us, she corresponds to Milton's Sin, the keeper of hell's gate.[1] Her particular sin is 'dark secret love', the associating of love with possession which causes Satan to think he loves Palamabron, and hence to want to take over his work. Leutha corresponds to the repentant harlot of Biblical symbolism: sin is redeemable, and hence Leutha's world, the

[1] Cf. M. 13:39 with *P. L.* ii, 760. Thomas Wright, *Life of William Blake*, I, 105, associates her in the personal allegory with Harriet Poole of Lavant; Erdman, *op. cit.*, 396, in the political allegory with Marie Antoinette.

matrix of our own, is providentially protected until the Last Judgement.

The moral of the Bard's Song is, first, that the culture Milton belonged to is in a desperate state: Palamabron still preserves his integrity, like Job, but is fighting for his life, and those for whom he works are increasingly pulled under the self-righteousness and callous indifference of Satan. Second, that Palamabron's pity and love, which leads him to make social friends of his spiritual enemies, is not strong enough to hold out. The three classes belong to the sexual threefold world of Beulah, not the human fourfold world of Eden, and hence are involved in the fallen world. Ololon gives what is intended to be a key to the argument when she says (referring to the fact that the Fall began in Beulah):

> Altho' our Human Power can sustain the severe contentions
> Of Friendship, our Sexual cannot, but flies into the Ulro.
> Hence arose all our terrors in Eternity.

The Bard's Song shocks those who recognize that it associates pity and love with guilt (M 14 : 48), but Milton understands. Milton had portrayed Christ as rejecting Classical wisdom in *Paradise Regained*, on the ground that if Christ were to exchange the prophetic tradition for it, he would get only a development of the kind of natural religion which exists in hell. Yet Milton, according to Blake's Preface, had not successfully resisted this temptation himself. In heaven he is still 'pond'ring the intricate mazes of Providence' (M. 2 : 17). The sinister image of the maze, and the deliberate recall of *P. L.* ii, 561, indicates that Milton is still sufficiently in the grip of natural religion to be without his emanation, which is partly his influence after death (M. 46 : 10), for the world still worships false gods (M. 15 : 14), and the results of doing so are painfully evident. So Milton resolves to return to the world in human form to bring about a dialectical opposition between imagination and nature, and stop the cycle of nature from turning. There is no question of 'reincarnation,' as Milton enters the body of a full-grown poet with a highly developed personality of his own, but Blake is adapting, whether he knew it or not, the Oriental myth of the Bodhisattva, the saint who voluntarily re-enters the world to help liberate it.

The process of return sends Milton into a 'vortex', the void outside existence which becomes a womb when entered (M. 48 : 37 f.).[1] The sons of Los are terrified at his approach, because Milton is journeying through chaos like his own Satan, and they assume that he is Satan. The chaos is simultaneously the chaos of the moral law, the labyrinthine desert, and the chaos of the natural law, the labyrinthine Newtonian universe. From the latter point of view Milton is a falling star or comet, the comet being here, as in *America* and *Europe*, the symbol of a new 'Eye' or phase of human fortunes, like the new star at the birth of Christ, which with fear of change perplexes monarchs. From the former point of view he is a pillar of fire, described in *America* as 'The fiery joy, that Urizen perverted to ten commands'.

Milton is repeating the journey of Moses in the wilderness, and the journey of Christ in *Paradise Regained*. Negatively, he

[1] Ololon's remark is repeated in the frontispiece to *Jerusalem*, in the newly discovered inscription referred to above. I have nothing to add to my explanation of the vortex in *Fearful Symmetry*, 350, except that its iconography is often serpentine: see the middle figure at the bottom of the plate of *America* beginning 'Albion's Angel stood beside the Stone of night'.

must preserve the 'wrath' of Rintrah, the total detachment that will split him off from Satan's world. Hence he must resist the temptation to cross the Jordan and enter 'Canaan' instead of the Promised Land, thereby turning the wheel of time around once more instead of stopping it. Positively, he must preserve the other side of wrath, the mercy (M. 25 : 34) or forgiveness of sins which withdraws completely from the movement of attack and revenge in history. He could easily become a new force in history, like Luther before him, another king of the wood who will last until destroyed by the next one (M. 43 : 30 ff.), but, like Shelley's Prometheus, he can redeem man only by renouncing all desire for revenge.

Again, he must recapitulate the struggle of the three classes, retaining his own form of a prophet while consolidating and destroying the Negation of the moral law (M. 22 : 20 ff.). Also he must repeat the Incarnation, in the sense of achieving an Adamic body, or a fallen human perspective, without falling prey to the Urizenic abstract vision. This is symbolized by the contest of Milton and Urizen on the banks of the sinister river Arnon, in which Milton kneads a shape of red clay (the meaning of the word Adam in Hebrew, and more or less of the word Milton in Greek) on icy water. The episode suggests Jacob's wrestling with the angel and Christ's healing the blind man with clay and spittle. We are not told just what relation this body has to the body of William Blake, but the process going on between the desert and the Promised Land is simultaneously going on between the sea and the Sussex coast, the mountains of the one (M. 19 : 16) being identical with the 'Rocks of Bognor' (M. 44 : 49) on the other.

The moral act which begins in wrath and ends in forgiveness is also an intellectual act. Besides the Adam, Noah, and Israel accounts of the fall and redemption of man, there is a fourth, the story told in the Book of Job, which Blake had begun to read in Hebrew.[1] The story of Job is the story of man, who suffers undeservedly because he falls into Satan's world. Satan cannot touch his real life (cf. M. 44 : 18 ff.) or imagination, but he is capable of arranging the conditions of a fallen world, and, like Jesus judging Adam in *Paradise Lost*, of compelling him to live in it. 'In the Book of Job,' Blake had said, 'Milton's Messiah is call'd Satan.' Eventually Job is enlightened by God, who points out to him the two vast monsters, behemoth and leviathan, the giant forms of fallen nature, and clearly identical with Satan, who in the meantime has disappeared from the action. The fourteenth and fifteenth plates of the Job series represent the difference between the 'Redeemed' and the full 'Reprobate' vision. In the former, Job and his wife are separated from the unfallen world, the frieze of angels, by a demiurge controlling the movements of the sun and the moon, while the acts of creation proceed around the margin. In the latter, behemoth and leviathan take up the lower part of the plate, and Job and his wife are above them. One is a threefold vision with the providentially protected cycle of nature in the middle; the other is the final contrast of Eden and Ulro. These two visions correspond roughly to the visions in *Milton* at the end of the first and of the second book respectively.

Milton finds in the world he returns to a crisis in history with the Napoleonic wars, a crisis in religion with the collapse of

[1] Letter to James Blake, Jan. 30, 1803. Of Blake's knowledge of the Hebrew Bible two examples will suffice. The phrase translated 'Lucifer, son of the morning' in Isa. xiv, 12, is in Hebrew *Helal ben Sahar*, which underlies the identification of Lucifer with 'Hillel' (M. 35 : 8) in a later plate. In Judges xviii, 30, the name Moses is written Manasseh, an editorial expurgation glanced at in M. 26: 6 (Tirzah was of the tribe of Manasseh).

Swedenborg and the failure of anyone to make a genuinely imaginative development out of the challenge of the Methodist movement, a crisis in philosophy with the dogmatic formulation of natural religion in contemporary Deism, and a crisis in art with the domination of 'the tame high finisher of paltry Blots' (M. 48 : 9). All these crises are negative signs of an imminent awakening, and have to be turned inside out by the imagination. Thus when Blake describes war as the treading of a winepress, he is not closing his eyes to its horror: he is seeing the wars of human life as the literal Word of God (M. 49 : 14), its natural or demonic parody, which in its inside-out or 'adverse' form (M. 29 : 9 ff.) becomes apocalyptic. The vision of Milton–Blake begins with the 'Wine-press on the Rhine' (M. 27 : 3), expands to the vision of art and science on Plate 30, and finally achieves the vision of time and space as the home, tent,[1] or tabernacle of man. At the end of Book One, the whole objective world is seen as a creation of Los, and is thereby transformed into a responsive emanation, the Beulah described at the opening of Book Two, from whence Ololon the milky way descends, like the angels descending Jacob's ladder (M. 39 : 35). The emanation retreats from anyone who seeks her in the outside world, but appears when the natural perspective is reversed; hence the paradox that although the object of Milton's journey is to seek Ololon, Ololon in fact seeks him.

Her journey differs from Milton's in that she traverses the created rather than the creating states, or the four emanation

[1] M. 31 : 4; the tent is the symbol of the fact that the City of God is movable. The tent is pyramidal in shape, the pyramid being its demonic parody, its stony frozen form (cf. the pyramidal shape of the shepherds' tents in one of Blake's *Nativity Ode* illustrations). Blake regarded the story of Sisera as a reminiscence of the fall of Albion, hence Albion is slain in his tent (M. 3 : 2).

worlds. The first of these is Beulah, the emanation of Eden; the next is called Alla, the 'night of Beulah' or world of dreams freed from what we should call a censor (M. 25 : 39 ff.). The third is the projection of our own world, single vision and Newton's sleep; the fourth is the nightmare or delirium world which can always be found below the third one, and inspires its constant panic and cruelty. Both are forms of Ulro, distinguished as Al-Ulro and Or-Ulro (M. 38 : 12 f.). Or-Ulro is the world from which Thel ran shrieking: Ololon has more courage, as well as the support of numbers.

As she comes down to 'Blake's Cottage at Felpham' (so labelled on Plate 40), the moment of vision is accomplished, the moment neither in time nor out of time which contains the whole of time, the 'Pulsation of the Artery' in which 'the Poet's Work is Done' (M. 31 : 1 ff.). As Satan splits off from Milton, and the female will from Ololon, we hear in the distance the 'Cry of the Poor Man' (M. 49 : 34), and the preparations for a greater awakening of humanity (cf. M. 4 : 21 ff.). In this expectant hush the poem ends, as quietly as *Paradise Regained* ends with the return of Christ to his mother, and one of the most gigantic imaginative achievements in English poetry comes to a controlled close.

V

The Theme and Structure of William Blake's Jerusalem

by

Karl Kiralis

The St. Lawrence University, Canton, New York (*U.S.A.*)

V

The Theme and Structure of William Blake's Jerusalem

THOUGH *Jerusalem* is generally considered to be one of the most enigmatic if not chaotic works produced by a major figure in English literature, actually William Blake explains its theme and structure within the work itself. The very nature of the structure, one of interfolded growth as described on plate 98, seems to have caused critics to shy away from a sufficient consideration of the basic form of the work.

In 1811, Southey dismissed the whole problem by calling what he saw of *Jerusalem* 'a perfectly mad poem'; Allen Cunningham scorned it as an 'animated absurdity'; Alexander Gilchrist turned Blake's own words—'Scattered upon the void in incoherent despair'—against the poem. Later nineteenth-century critics—except those like William Michael Rossetti, who dismissed the prophetic books simply as the work of a madman—were somewhat kinder but actually of little help. Although there were still many like Henry G. Hewlett, who called *Jerusalem* 'as unreadable an amalgam as is to be found in our literature', Swinburne described it ecstatically as a 'great book, . . . rich, vehement, and subtle beyond all works of Blake; the chosen crown and treasured fruit of his strange labor'. But this is just Swinburne in one rapture, for in another mood he laments 'in earnest' that the 'externals of this poem are too incredibly grotesque—the mythological plan too incomparably tortuous—to be fit for any detailed coherence of remark'. E. J. Ellis and W. B. Yeats in a three-volume *Works of William Blake* were the first to come truly to grips with *Jerusalem* in their plate-by-plate analysis. While they made some happy discoveries, even they concluded that the arrangement of *Jerusalem* is that of a 'scrapbook' and the story a 'paradox'.

In the criticism of the twentieth century, S. Foster Damon calls *Jerusalem* a storehouse rather than a vehicle of thought. He does suggest, however, a possible form, one of a great symphony, in respect to its 'definite statement of themes, . . . interweaving voices, . . . and involved development-passages of huge emotional sweep and change'. Northrop Frye, though alluding to the analogy of the symphony, is intent on showing *Jerusalem*'s concern with man's cosmic history as Blake interprets it from the Bible. Frye contends that *Jerusalem* is a 'recreation of the Bible' fitting 'the parts of that vast and chaotic book together with a more than theological precision'. Bernard Blackstone considers *Jerusalem* 'a reinterpretation of Christian doctrine' emphasizing 'self-forgiveness', and 'feels' it to be a unity, despite its many windings, with Jesus as the unifying force. David V. Erdman finds 'greater thematic unity than in the earlier epics' but 'not so much orderliness . . . as the division into four equal chapters might lead us to suspect'. The thematic unity is that of 'peace without vengeance' when set in the contemporary frame of reference of 'the years of Napoleon's decline and fall and of the triumph of British and German arms'. In view of Blake's richness, it is not surprising that most critics have chosen to treat other aspects of *Jerusalem* than the relations between theme and structure. Even the recent and long-awaited full-length commentary on *Jerusalem* by Joseph Wicksteed slights the structure by merely describing the poem as a 'many-sided and all-comprehensive Epic Drama' with a male 'Time-Trinity' and a female 'Space-Trinity' as 'structurally necessary to the plot'.[1]

This brief survey indicates that no one has pointed out that Blake's own words present a comprehensible explanation of the theme and the structure as organically related elements. Many have noted—Alexander Gilchrist was the first[2]—that Blake gives the broad outline of his theme at the outset:

> Of the Sleep of Ulro! and of the passage through
> Eternal Death! and of the awaking to Eternal Life.
> This theme calls me. (*Jerusalem* 4 : 1–3)[3]

[1] Henry Crabb Robinson, *Diary and Reminiscences*, ed. T. Sadler (London, 1869). I, 338. Allan Cunningham, *The Lives of the Most Eminent British Painters, Sculptors, and Architects*, 2nd ed. (London, 1830), II, 161. Alexander Gilchrist, *Life of William Blake*, revised ed. (London, 1880), I, 227–8, 238–9. William Michael Rossetti, 'Prefatory Memoir', *The Poetical Works of William Blake*, Aldine ed. (London, 1905), pp. cxxi–cxxii. Henry G. Hewlett, 'Imperfect Genius: William Blake', *The Contemporary Review*, XXVIII (Oct., 1876), 779. A. C. Swinburne, *William Blake, a Critical Essay* (London, 1868), p. 294, p. 282. E. J. Ellis and W. B. Yeats, *The Works of William Blake* (London, 1893), II, 176. S. Foster Damon, *William Blake: His Philosophy and Symbols* (New York, 1924), reprinted 1947, p. 195. Northrop Frye, *Fearful Symmetry, a Study of William Blake* (Princeton, 1947), p. 360. Bernard Blackstone, *English Blake* (Cambridge, 1949), pp. 158–9. David V. Erdman, *Blake, Prophet against Empire: a Poet's Interpretation of the History of His Own Times* (Princeton, 1954), p. 427. Joseph Wicksteed, *William Blake's Jerusalem* (London, 1954), pp. 6, 15–16.

[2] Gilchrist, I, 231. P. Berger seems to have been the first to try to explain how Blake states his theme directly, but his discussion of *Jerusalem* arrives at the conclusion that it cannot live as a whole literary work but only in its parts. *William Blake, Mysticisme et Poésie* (Paris, 1907), pp. 400–412.

[3] All references to Blake's writing are based on the one-volume edition of Sir Geoffrey Keynes—*Poetry and Prose of William Blake* (London, 1948). Although Sir Geoffrey's punctuation is no longer considered as final—see H. M. Margoliouth, *William Blake* (London, 1951), p. 175—I find it adequate for my quotations in this paper.

Oft-quoted also is the passage in which Blake states his purpose:

I rest not my great task!
To open the Eternal Worlds, to open the immortal Eyes
Of Man inwards into the Worlds of Thought, into Eternity
Ever expanding in the Bosom of God, the Human Imagination. (5 : 17–20)

No one, however, has yet observed that Blake in plate 98, while ostensibly describing the conversations of the Four Zoas as 'they walked / To and fro in Eternity', in effect is again presenting his theme and structure.

And they conversed together in Visionary forms dramatic which bright
Redounded from their Tongues in thunderous majesty, in Visions
In new Expanses, creating exemplars of Memory and of Intellect,
Creating Space, Creating Time, according to the wonders Divine
Of Human Imagination throughout all the Three Regions immense
Of Childhood, Manhood & Old Age; & all the tremendous unfathomable Non Ens
Of Death was seen in regenerations terrific or complacent, varying
According to the subject of discourse; & every Word and every Character
Was Human according to the Expansion or Contraction, the Translucence or

Opakeness of Nervous fibres: such was the variation of Time & Space
Which vary according as the Organs of Perception vary; & they walked
To & fro in Eternity as One Man, reflecting each in each & clearly seen
And seeing, according to fitness & order. (98 : 28–40)

This passage contains lines which effectively hint at the form and substance of the poem. In fact, every phrase in this passage is intended to clarify some aspect of the work, especially the theme and structure. I will discuss at some length the key phrases—'the Three Regions immense / Of Childhood, Manhood & Old Age', and 'One Man, reflecting each in each'—but first to attend the minute particulars in the order in which they appear in this passage: 'Visionary forms dramatic' describes the actors in the drama of man's fall and resurrection. They are 'Visionary' since the old classical, religious, and philosophical symbolism had for Blake become too closely associated with the shadowy world, the world of death, Ulro. They are made dramatic by Blake's frequent placing of them in direct opposition: Vala debates angrily with Jerusalem (plates 20, 79–80); Albion with both of them (21–23); Los, despite his own domestic difficulties (86–88), continually attempts to save Albion, who refuses to be saved; Jerusalem questions the ways of Jesus (60–62). There is also internal conflict: Los undergoes a personal struggle with his rational self (8–12) and with his sexual desire (82, 86); Albion suffers within (23, 24, 28, 38, etc.), as does Jerusalem (78–79). The 'exemplars of Memory' are the archetypes not hidden from the corporeal understanding, such as the character of Albion or of Joseph;

those 'of Intellect' are addressed to the intellectual powers and include Urthona, Erin, and Reuben. The 'exemplars' could also well refer to the many aphorisms in *Jerusalem*. An exemplar of memory, for example, contrasts the attitude of the public to the peaceful man and to the soldier in time of war:

> Ashamed to give Love openly to the piteous & merciful Man,
> Counting him an imbecile mockery, but the Warrior
> They adore & his revenge cherish with the blood of the Innocent. (67 : 19–21)

One exemplar of the many in *Jerusalem* which rouse the intellectual powers to act may be:

> What is a Wife & what is a Harlot? What is a Church & What
> Is a Theatre? are they Two & not One? can they Exist Separate?
> Are not Religion & Politics the Same Thing? Brotherhood is Religion. (57 : 8–10)

The creation of space and time according to the imagination was necessary since the concept of time and space belongs to the world of mortality. This imaginative creation explains Blake's notorious misuse (by rational standards) of chronology and topography. He simply would not be enslaved by another man's system. The 'Non Ens / Of Death' are the non-entities, by eternal standards, of the material world, such as physical war and its industry, or conventional religions. The explanation that the 'regenerations' of the 'Non Ens' vary 'according to the subject of discourse' is most readily appreciated by referring back to Blake's awareness of the need of expression to suit the subject matter: 'Every word and every letter is studied and put into its fit place; the terrific numbers are reserved for the terrific parts, the mild & gentle for the mild & gentle parts, and the prosaic for inferior parts; all are necessary to each other' (3 : 43–46). The degree of successful communication is directly proportionate to the individual reader's perceptiveness, which naturally will vary since both 'Nervous fibres' and 'Organs of Perception' vary.

The two crucial phrases—'the Three Regions immense / Of Childhood, Manhood & Old Age', and 'One Man, reflecting each in each'—require fuller explanation than the other lines of this passage. It has often been noted that, after the first chapter, which is addressed 'To the Public', each chapter is directed at a specific group: Chapter II to the Jews, III to the Deists, and IV to the Christians.[1] What have escaped notice are the progressive relationships of these three religions to 'the Three Regions immense / Of Childhood, Manhood & Old Age', for it can be demonstrated that Blake, in *Jerusalem*, considers the Jews to be in a state of mental childhood, the deists in manhood, and the Christians either in maturity if the theoretical potential of Christianity is realized or in senility if it is not. Earlier in *Jerusalem* (plate 14), when describing the whole body of his work, Blake points out (l. 25) that 'every one has the three regions, Childhood, Manhood & Age'. Perhaps Blake changed 'Age' to 'Old Age' when he realized that Christianity

[1] Ellis and Yeats were the first to note the intentional fourfold division of *Jerusalem* and suggest the states of creation, redemption, judgment, and regeneration as the respective titles of each of the four chapters (II, 176). Margoliouth even organizes his summary of the poem on the basis of the fact that each chapter, after the first 'To the Public', is addressed to a particular group and its errors. (Pages 151–170.)

must be truly realized and practiced before it can be considered the State of Maturity; otherwise the discrepancy between preaching forgiveness and practicing vengeance under the name of Christianity would be indicative of senility. The child and the Jew, on the other hand, both believe, preach, and practice the strict justice of the eye-for-an-eye philosophy, with no pretense of forgiveness to shield their actions.

In broad outline, the progressive growth is illustrated by the fact that Chapter I is the general introduction, the prelude or overture, to the other three chapters. It contains the story of the fall and considers, in brief, the forces which would help and those which would hinder man as described with variation and elaboration in the subsequent chapters. After describing the fall (plates 20–24, especially 24 : 60), Chapter I ends in such confusion that Jesus is called upon to establish order by the creation of states which will 'take away the imputation of Sin' to individuals (25 : 12–13). This creation is to result in a set path through Ulro or Error (cf. 4 : 1–3), whose three chief states are described in the following three chapters, each of which is a critical summary of the philosophical errors of a particular state, II of Judaism, III of deism, and IV of Christianity.

At the end of each of the first three chapters there is definite preparation for the succeeding chapter. The call for states at the end of Chapter I is fulfilled in II, but the call to take away the sense of guilt—'the Remembrance of Sin'—at the end of II (50 : 24–30) is answered in III only by Jesus' showing how the sense of guilt could be removed—that is, by the mutual granting of unconditional forgiveness (61). At the end of III, Blake emphasizes the necessity for the existence of the cycle of twenty-seven churches—that is, Blake's detailed analysis of the three basic states as they begin with Adam and end with Luther (75). At the end, man has completed his earthly progression through the states, and more specifically through the twenty-seven churches, to eternity. The work closes on the hope that the cycle from mundane to eternal life will continue (99 : 2–4).

Each system builds upon the ruins of the preceding one in the course of man's spiritual or intellectual growth. At the end of Chapter I, Albion, in self-guilt, having denied Jerusalem and cursed mankind, has died without hope, but in the arms of Jesus (plates 23, 24, especially 24 : 60). At the beginning of II, alive as punisher and judge, Albion creates his own system of justice and truth, Judaism, under the influence of the tree of moral virtue, which he names the law of God (28).

Blake's reasons for considering Judaism as the region of childhood in man's spiritual development are probably threefold. First and most apparently, the Christian church considers Judaism as the earliest religion. Second, in human terms, the child must learn justice before mercy; he must learn to recognize and abhor sin before he can learn to forgive it. Third, and most basic, is the fact that essential to Judaism is (the error of) moral law—the adherence to moral law being considered an adherence to God—as evidenced most obviously by the Ten Commandments. On this depends the entire system of human justice—the accuser, the judge, and the executioner being Blake's infernal trinity. It is this strict, codified system which Jesus was to abrogate.

A clear indication of God's dissatisfaction with Judaism is the deluge of plate 36. That man was not content with Judaism is made clear by Albion's readiness to die (plate 39) as the result of his fear of his fellow man and his conviction that God had forsaken him. The final indication that Judaism must give way to another state is Albion's death without hope near the end of the chapter (plate 48), but again he dies in the Saviour's arms.

In human terms, it is usual for the child as he develops into manhood to cast off supernaturalism and to enter into the state of agnosticism. The agnostics of Blake's time called themselves deists because they postulated the existence of God, even though he never interfered with the mechanical operations of the material universe which he had created. Blake's opposition to deism appears in his first engraved plates—'There is no Natural Religion' and 'All Religions are One' (ca. 1788). Now in Chapter III of *Jerusalem* he shows that deism is a natural state in the progress of every intellectual person. He shows how it develops from the Hebraic philosophy its own shortsighted system which preserves the Jewish adaption of the pagan division of all things into virtues and vices.

Near the beginning of Chapter III, Albion is described as having fallen because of his reason; moreover, now reason proclaims itself as God (54). Shortly (57) Albion is plowed in with the dead, but his spectre (i.e. his reason) survives. In this chapter, the flood comes early (57 : 3–5), and Albion for the most part remains dead or fallen; however, there is definite promise at the end of his awakening (75 : 25, 26). Quite aptly, Vala as natural religion is the crowned figure of the frontispiece.[1] Bacon, Newton, and Locke are Blake's logical choices for his evil trinity of deists, although Voltaire and Rousseau do not escape his wrath (see plate 52). Since he looked on

[1] The fact that the figures are not named in any of the copies of *Jerusalem* while there exist three separate plates labelling the figures—see Ruthven Todd, ed., *Alexander Gilchrist's Life of William Blake* (London, 1945), p. 202—suggests that Blake is rousing his readers' faculties.

deism as essentially an English creation, Blake emphasizes the English antiquities (i.e. the druidic remains and Arthurian characters) in Chapter III.

Chapter IV, addressed 'To the Christians', is the last of the three stages in the progress through eternal death. As agnosticism developed from reaction to Judaism, so Christianity develops from reaction to agnosticism. Of course there are many individuals so sunk in the waters of materialism and so deluded by the faith in reason alone that they never aspire to this stage, but, historically and practically speaking, in the western world they are the exceptions. Blake shows that official or historical Christianity also has its errors which must be recognized to be cast off. The outstanding flaw of historical Christianity, according to Blake, is the over-importance given to women. While he elevates woman from the position of household drudge to an essential part of man's being, indeed his very inspiration, at the same time he recognizes her jealousy, not only of his attitude towards other women but even of his life work, and of what she apprehends of eternity.

Chapter IV, then, opens with Albion's sons crowning Vala, whom they name Rahab, as queen, while Jerusalem lies enchained with her foundations in dust. That is, a temporal and material religion, the religion of rational morality, appears in the guise of Christianity while the true spirit of Christianity lies captured and in ruins (plate 78). Although at first refusing to take definite form (80 : 51, 52) for fear that the delusions be discovered, Rahab finally appears within the Covering Cherub (89 : 52, 53), Blake's conception of the antichrist, the externals of religion rather than its internal spirit.[1] Shortly thereafter

[1] Ezekiel's description of the Prince of Tyrus (Ezekiel xxviii. 11–16) was generally accepted as the description of Satan himself. To Blake, Ezekiel's

(93 : 18–26) Los can announce the 'Signal of the Morning' now that the forces of error have taken form. Thereupon Albion's wife, Britannia, confesses her jealousy and her use of chastity and moral law to control man (94 : 22–26):

> O pitious Sleep, O pitious Dream! O God, O God awake! I have slain
> In Dreams of Chastity & Moral Law: I have Murdered Albion!
>
> . . . .
>
> I have Slain him in my Sleep with the Knife of the Druid. O England!
> O all ye Nations of the Earth, behold ye the Jealous Wife!
>
> (94 : 22–26)

After her willing submission, Albion is prepared to absorb the basic tenet of Christianity, forgiveness (96), and once he is truly convinced, he becomes whole again (96) and is able to annihilate the Covering Cherub (98). So at last the warring Zoas are again in harmony; all men have become one in Albion: man and woman became one when Britannia entered Albion's bosom. Finally God and man are one, and everything on earth has become humanized. Having reached full maturity, man, precisely because he is free, will again fall into error, but with

'Covering Cherub' was associated with the Cherub on the Ark, whose wings protected the sacred things within. Thus it became a symbol for dogma, which is an intelligent (cherubic) formula devised for the preservation of the truth. But when the truth is forgotten, the formula acquires new power, and being now meaningless may become the contradiction of the very truth it was intended to preserve. As Blake says in *The Four Zoas*, 'Christ's crucifix shall be made an excuse for Executing Criminals'.

his freedom (Jerusalem) and with the help of the poet he will renew the cycle from earthly to eternal life.[1]

Although there has been a progressive growth from Judaism to Christianity, in a way there has also been regressive growth in order to give a body to error that it may be destroyed.

This is well illustrated by the gradual gain of power and at the same time the exposure of the female will. In Chapter I the female will is merely suggested. We learn only that the poet's emanation—his inspiration, 'yet his wife until the sleep of Death is passed' (14 : 14)—has painfully divided from him (6 : 3 and 17 : 47 ff.). Chapter IV (86–88) contains nearly a full scale debate between the poet, who insists on dominance that he may do the work of eternity, and his wife, who attempts to weave a 'Female Tabernacle for Moral Law' that 'God himself [may] become a Male subservient to the Female'. (88 : 19–21) The cancer grows gradually. In Chapter I, for fear that their beauty will make him forget his eternal task (17 : 1–15), Los sends out his spectre against the daughters of Albion, who hide in cold chastity 'terrified by undisguis'd desire'. In II, man humbles himself to Vala as if she were God (29), and Vala demands man's obedience on the ground that she alone is beauty and love (33). Then the female will is

[1] The inevitability of the cycle is made clear in plate 99:

> All Human Forms identified, even Tree, Metal, Earth & Stone: all
> Human Forms identified, living, going forth & returning wearied
> Into the Planetary lives of Years, Months, Days & Hours; reposing,
> And then Awaking into his Bosom in the Life of Immortality.
>
> And I heard the Name of their Emanations: they are named Jerusalem.
>
> (plate 99)

The cycle is renewed in plate 100, for the poet (the central figure) with the aid of his reason and inspiration is again at work to help man, who seems already to have fallen again as indicated by the prominent druidic ruins in the background.

identified and condemned by the poet himself (34). In Chapter III the daughters have become so powerful—'what may Woman be / To have power over Man from Cradle to corruptible Grave'—that Los, bemoaning Albion's creation of a female will, steels himself to challenge them without fear (56).

Another clear example of this regressive growth, particularly that of Vala, begins in I, where comparatively brief mention is made of the fact that Albion enfolds his dying self within Vala's veil of moral law (23 : 35 f.). In II Los states that Albion has entered the loins, the place of last judgment in Vala's bosom (30 : 38 f.). In III Vala is described at length and identified as the eternal form of Rahab (70 : 31), natural morality (or moral virtue—39 : 10). At the outset (52) Rahab was named as the very soul of deism; at the end of III (75), to prepare for the final chapter, as the Whore of Babylon she is at the core of the twenty-seven religions. Vala-Rahab unites with the spectre (reason) in 64, though the formal building of deism is not erected until 66. There is bare mention of the daughters of Albion uniting into Rahab and Tirzah in plate 5 and in the person of Gwendolen in 34, but in Chapter III their technique as Rahab and Tirzah is quite fully explained (67–69). First Blake makes clear that the tabernacle of Rahab and Tirzah, which has spread over the whole earth, arises from the sufferings of their victims (67). The sufferings come about first through Tirzah, for she assumes the role of the temptress exciting but then denying love to man, who frustrated becomes cruel and vents his anger in war (67–68).

I am drunk with unsatiated love,
I must rush again to War, for the Virgin has frown'd & refus'd.

> Sometimes I curse & sometimes bless thy fascinating beauty.
> Once Man was occupied in intellectual pleasures & energies,
> But now my Soul is harrow'd with grief & fear & love & desire,
> And now I hate & now I love, & Intellect is no more.
> There is no time for anything but the torments of love & desire. (68 : 62–68)

The role of Rahab is to provide man with some satisfaction by 'forming a commerce to sell Loves' in a religion of chastity and moral law (69). But even in marriage, as is stated in II,

> a Man dare hardly to embrace
> His own Wife for the terrors of Chastity that they call
> By the name of Morality . . . (36 : 45–47)

The consequences of the belief in the virginity of Mary foster the female will's attempt to impose its code. In III, Blake interpolated plate 61 in the hope of dispelling this belief in Mary's virginity by relating what he must have considered a much more Christian interpretation. Joseph, though at first angry with Mary since she was pregnant before their marriage, finally forgives her. He gains this knowledge of unconditional forgiveness with the help of an angel, after Mary has argued that had she been pure she could never have tasted of the 'sweets / Of the Forgiveness of Sin'.

In general then the female will, with its code of chastity and moral law—the 'cruelties of holiness'—is discussed at greater length in III than in either of the preceding chapters.[1]

It should be clear by now that Blake has been gradually revealing the power and the error of the female will that it may

[1] Beyond the examples already mentioned, a full scale analysis of the female will by Los appears on 56, Vala triumphs 'in pride of holiness' over

be destroyed—'to be an Error and to be Cast out is part of God's design' (*Vision of the Last Judgment*, p. 84). First the error must fully expose itself in Chapter IV as the source of the perversion of Christianity. At the beginning of the chapter, Vala is crowned queen 'to destroy the Lamb & usurp the Throne of God' in order to indicate that the temporal religion of moral virtue has replaced Christianity. Vala-Rahab refuses to take definite form, however, as she spreads over the earth; but as if to make her take form Blake presents four definite scenes: the debate between Jerusalem and Vala (79–80), the attempt of Gwendolen and Cambel to dominate Hyle and Hand (80–82), the struggle of Los with Enitharmon (86–88), and finally the admission of guilt by 'the Jealous Wife', Britannia, whose confession, along with divine help, results in man's awakening.

In the Jerusalem–Vala episode, the female will is discussed in generalized terms. That is, Jerusalem (the city and the concept) in ruins bemoans the loss of paradise as the result of Vala's moral virtue and delusive beauty, which have ensnared man and made Jerusalem seemingly helpless. Ignoring Jerusalem's statement that 'Humanity is far above Sexual Organization', Vala freely admits that she must preserve delusion to preserve herself. She further maintains that Luvah (the love which is now perverted) has ordered her to embalm man in moral laws. These generalized concepts are particularized and activated in

Jerusalem in 60; Vala's veil, which has been cast into the Atlantic 'to catch the Souls of the Dead' in I, and has been suggested as forming the Mundane Shell in II (42:78–81), is more definitely described as forming the earthly limits (59). Further, Vala is forthright in 64 in her scorn of the male, even though Los attacks her attitude, and Vala is the spirit behind the crucifixion of Luvah (65–7).

both the Gwendolen–Cambel and Los–Enitharmon episodes. Cambel and Gwendolen attempt to form two of the sons of Albion to their wills by their use of sex and moral virtue. Gwendolen even goes so far as to instruct the other daughters in the ways of woman: ensnare the man by love and then refuse him by pleading chastity. These daughters fail, however, for Gwendolen's technique reduces man to his lowest form, the headless and heartless worm, from which woman flees. The struggle of the poet with his wife or inspiration is the most intimate and most detailed treatment of the female will in the chapter and for that matter in all of *Jerusalem*. The poet, obsessed by his loins, asks his wife to relieve his torment that he may return to his great task. Enitharmon answers that this is a woman's world and she will utilize his desire for her own purposes. Although the poet needs his inspiration to achieve brotherhood with man through intellectual discussion, he defies Enitharmon. She threatens to create a tabernacle of chastity and moral virtue that will make even God subservient to woman. Then Blake explains that at the basis of this contention between male and female is reason—that is, it is rational that woman try to control man in her fashion if society is to maintain itself. In eternity, however, woman realizes the error of the use of chastity and moral law, as Britannia does on her awakening. Prior to her awakening, however, Vala-Rahab has been given definite form within the Covering Cherub (89), and the patent worship by rational forces of Babylon or Vala-Rahab is the 'Signal of the Morning'. Before man can truly complete his cycle to eternity, he must annihilate the Covering Cherub.[1]

[1] Other examples of the growth structure do not call for such extended treatment. I present them here for those who would read with text in hand.

If the structure of growth is comprehended, the other key phrase, 'One Man, reflecting each in each', should be readily understandable, for the very nature of growth involves reflection. As the child is father of the man and each age reflects characteristics of the foregoing ones, so the chapters of *Jerusalem* reflect one another but at the same time remain a unit as the child, youth, and mature man are 'One Man'. The simplest illustration of reflection in *Jerusalem* is the fact that the strict

---

Chapter I contains the germ of what occurs later in *Jerusalem* somewhat as an infant possesses the nascent characteristics that become active in the child, the youth, and the mature man. In plate 5, for example, in his description of the shrunken finite world, Blake simply alludes to events which are fully developed later: the suffering of Jerusalem's children is described in 43: 60 and 78–80, the sons of Albion attempting to destroy Albion's humanity and Golgonooza in 32, 43, 49, 70, 74, and 79. In 5, Blake even lists (lines 24–26) what he intends to consider: the building of the City of Art (which is in process in 10–13, 16, 53, and 73, and completed in IV—cf. 83, 86, 88, 98); the terrors of abstract philosophy (with which he deals throughout, but especially in 10, 55, 70, 74, 78, 91); and the deeds of the sons and daughters of Albion (which are too numerous to be cited). Also in I there is such obvious preparation as the statement of the theme (the passage through eternal death to eternity), the call for forgiveness (in 3), which is stressed throughout and fulfilled gloriously near the end (97), the poet's call for man to awake (4) as he does in 95, and the poet's prophecy that 'all Albion's injuries shall cease' (7: 55), as they do (95 ff.). There are more subtle indications as well. For example, the brief notation that Hand and Hyle are 'rooted into Jerusalem by a fibre/Of strong revenge' (15: 1–2) is clarified in 80, where Cambel uses the fibres of Hand to weave Jerusalem a body repugnant to the Lamb; the bare statement that Gwendolen and Cambel weave 'webs of war and of/Religion to involve all Albion's sons' (7: 44–5) is quite fully developed in 58, 63–66, and 80–82; and the very phrase describing Enitharmon's division from Los into a 'red Globe of blood' (17: 51) is repeated (86: 52) and further explained.

Although the major characters, Los, Albion, Jerusalem, and Vala, appear in Chapter I, they are more fully developed in the subsequent chapters in

code of justice and moral law of the Jews reappears in deism and even in Christianity until it is fully recognized and cast off. This reflection pattern also helps absolve Blake of the charge that he is needlessly repetitious. The reason why Albion turns or flees from the divine vision in each chapter while Los constantly fears that man will forsake the divine vision and attempts to prevent him from so doing is that in each stage of history, as Blake conceives it, man does forsake the divine vision while the creative artist fears for him and tries to help

---

keeping with the idea and structure of growth. Jerusalem and Vala, for example, are characterized in 18–23, but they are expanded upon in 31, 33, 34, 60, 62, 64, 65, 78–80, and in 86, 89 they are compared practically point by point. Secondary characters such as Erin and Reuben are lightly treated in I, but play increasingly important roles later. Erin is perfected in Los' furnaces in 11, but her role is negligible until 48–50, where she summarizes the ills of Ulro before her rainbow appears (50: 22) as the promise of the resurrection of the body. In III, Erin is the last to be divided among the tribes of Israel (72) and her youthful form, Dinah, arises from the Four Zoas. In IV the loving emanations concenter in her 'majestic form' (86: 45), so that later (88: 33) she becomes part of a world with Los and his children. Her final appearance (94: 13) finds her guarding Albion in his tomb just before he awakes. Reuben enroots his brethren in 15 so that he is able in the succeeding chapters to represent all the tribes of Israel or the vegetative man (36: 23–4). He plays no part in I, but in II his senses are limited and he wanders frustrated and in doubt (34, 36). In III he flees and continues to wander aimlessly (63, 64, 68, 69, 72) and at one point is admired and punished in turn by the daughters of Albion (74: 33 ff.). In IV it is clear that he wanders in the big cities of the earth (84: 13, 14) as well as in Biblical lands, but Los appears finally to put an end to his wanderings by leading him into Canaan (85), here a moonlit, temporal existence—probably representing marriage. Ideally this is all we should hear of him, but he reappears being punished by the sons and daughters of Albion (90). (I ignore the reference to 93: 8, for there Reuben is not a character as he is elsewhere in *Jerusalem*, but rather used simply in a Biblical simile.)

him. Man's falling in each of the first three chapters [1] and the floods in II and III (36 : 39, 40 and 57 : 3–5) can be similarly explained. That is, the fall continues from its apparent beginning in Chapter I, but in II it occurs to illustrate that Judaism is not the true religion and in III to show that deism is not. Other 'reflections' include the presence in each chapter of the description of the fallen and unfallen worlds, the contrast of Jerusalem and Vala, Jesus' successive appearances and promises of help, the similar unveiled attacks upon conventional religion, war, war industry, and the ills of the Industrial Revolution, the repetition of the dangers and workings of the female will, and the reiteration of the need for liberty, the forgiveness of sin, and distinguishing the state from the individual.

I have concentrated on showing how Blake carries out his own explanation of *Jerusalem*'s theme and structure. It could be argued, however, that enough unanswered problems exist to indicate that Blake's explanation is the statement of his ideal objective, one which is not completely realized. In view of the fact that Blake established for his own purposes three stages of man's historical development, it would be expected that he concern himself with each stage in turn—that is, consider the Jews in II, the contemporary situation in III, and Christianity in IV. The daughters of Albion—whose names, except that of Gwinefred, are derived from the histories of Geoffrey and of Milton—play such a major role in IV that Blake may have had in mind the chivalric code in which the female will reigned. But he also had in mind the Jews, for frequent reference is made to the twelve tribes of Israel and the places associated

[1] Chapter I—24: 60; Chapter II—39: 16–23, 47: 17–48: 4; Chapter III—54: 6–8, 57: 12–16, 62: 2, 15, and cf. 75: 25–27.

with them, and the deists, as made evident by his references to Bacon, Newton, and Locke and to the English antiquities that he associates with deism. The situation is similarly confused in the other chapters, so much so that the pattern of reflection cannot be consistently applied. For example, Scofield and Kox, Blake's contemporaries, are referred to three times in Chapter II and Gwendolen six times in III. In this respect then Blake is walking up and down in man's history and 'to & fro' in eternity: that is, all the events are present before him; he selects from them to please his own imagination, and not so much to satisfy our rational minds as to awaken our intellectual faculties.

Another charge that might be levelled against Blake's execution of the structure of growth is the fact that not all of the individual chapters have any apparent plan of growth. We might expect, for example, that in each chapter man would go through his course of error and then fall or die at the end of the chapter, as occurs in broad outline in I and II, or that the error be gradually exposed and cast out as it is in IV. But even though some planning is evident in these chapters, the time and space shifts, the once mentioned but not explained characters or symbols, the 'reflections' and flashbacks, the puzzling details and epigrams, the lengthy though necessary direct explanations, and the various seemingly irrelevant diatribes do not make for a clear and definite design of growth. And in III, which, in view of its many interpolations, seems to have given Blake even more trouble than Chapter II with its two arrangements, the status of Albion is quite confusing. In the first place he seems to have fallen at the beginning (54 : 6–8) rather than at the end of the chapter; then, a little later (57 : 12–16), he is plowed in with the dead as he 'fled from the divine vision';

yet even so, Los later fears that he will fall (71 : 58–60). Although there is promise of Albion's awakening at the end (75 : 25–27), his awaking is also prophesied earlier by Jerusalem (62 : 2, 15). Whereas in I Blake lists events he will write about and then develops them later in the work, in III (74) he gives a longer list of occurrences, not all of which are developed either before or later in the work. Also in 74 he gives a more detailed but certainly much more confusing explanation of his theme as compared with his original statement of it.

It seems fair to conclude that Blake in *Jerusalem* was at times willfully obscure, but only in the sense that he was attempting to stimulate his readers' imaginations that they might apprehend and appreciate what he felt could not be expressed in rational terms. At other times it is unfortunate that he could not simply erase or interline, but the magnitude of his task—after all *Jerusalem* is Blake's *Divine Comedy*, *Paradise Lost*, and *Paradise Regained* in condensed form—makes Blake's failures forgivable. My main purpose, however, has been to show that he did intend a plan and to show how far he carried it out. In view of the direct statement of his theme early and late in the work, the division of the work into four distinct parts with a prose address to each and a frontispiece to the whole and to each of the last three chapters, the clear explanation of a structure of growth in the summary passage of plate 98, and his earlier claim that all his works contain the three regions of childhood, manhood, and age, his intention of a definite structure seems well established.[1]

[1] I am much indebted to both S. Foster Damon, who has greatly encouraged my study of Blake, and David V. Erdman, who has given me most valuable advice on this essay.

VI

William Blake and Hindu Creation Myths

by

Piloo Nanavutty
(*India*)

VI

William Blake and Hindu Creation Myths

The face of Truth remains hidden behind a circle of gold. Unveil it, O God of Light, that I, who love the true, may see.[1]

THIS PRAYER, FROM the *Isha Upanishad*, would have appealed to Blake, for he spent his life unveiling the face of Truth in his poetry and his art displaying a power and beauty beyond the dream of thought.

As a poet and a visionary he was sensitive to all he read and saw. Yet it should never be forgotten that Blake is first and foremost a Christian visionary, so if he borrows a Hindu symbol, such as that of the Blue Lotus for instance, he places it not in a Hindu but a Christian setting.[2] In that lovely lyric, 'The Sick Rose' in *The Songs of Experience*, he reverses a popular emblem tradition in order to bring out his own distinctive vision of love and suffering.[3] His use of the various Hindu creation myths, well known in the eighteenth century, is similarly conditioned.

Before examining some of these myths it is but fair to satisfy the legitimate curiosity of the modern reader who wishes to know the main sources from which knowledge of India came to Europe in Blake's day.

The earliest accounts of India come from the Christian

[1] J. Mascaro, *Himalayas of the Soul*, Wisdom of the East Series, London, 1937, p. 1.

[2] Piloo Nanavutty, 'A Title Page in Blake's Illustrated Genesis MS.'. *Journal of the Warburg and Courtauld Institutes*, Vol. X, 1947, pp. 114 seq.

[3] Piloo Nanavutty, 'Blake and Emblem Literature', *Journal of the Warburg and Courtauld Institutes*, Vol. XV, 1952, Nos. 3–4, pp. 158–161.

missionaries, Dutch, Spanish, English, French and German. Their voluminous writings, starting from Abraham Roger's *De open Deure* (Leyden, 1651),[1] were eagerly read by all and sundry. These writings whetted the appetite of travellers, and a stream of publications on the manners, customs, ceremonies, religious and political institutions of India, Japan, China and Indonesia, followed.

The popular and rather garbled accounts given by missionaries and travellers stimulated scholars and critics like Sir William Jones, Sir Charles Wilkins, Colebrooke and others to study Indian life and thought more seriously. The periodical, *Asiatic Researches*, was firmly established, and relevant problems discussed in its pages.[2]

Actual translations of Indian texts, however, were comparatively few, but read with all the greater avidity for this reason. The most important among these may be mentioned. The earliest were two small volumes entitled *L'Ezour Vedam*, published anonymously at Yverdon in 1778. They were translated into German by J. Ith and published at Bern the following year. Accepted as genuine, it was not until 1822 that the authenticity of the work was exposed when Francis Ellis wrote his 'Account of a discovery of a modern imitation of the Vedas' in the *Asiatic Researches* of that year.

[1] Roger himself did not go to India, but worked in Palicat and Batavia where he met Indians resident there. Two French translations of his work are extant, while M. V. de la Croze, J. R. Sinner and others copied extensively from *De open Deure*.

[2] Sir W. Jones on the Vedas, *Asiatic Researches*, Vol. III, pp. 47 seq.
Wilford on the Puranas, *ibid.*, Vol. V. pp. 244 seq.
Colebrooke compares Puranas and Vedas, *ibid.*, Vol. VII, pp. 284 seq.
Bentley on the Puranas, *ibid.*, Vol. VIII, p. 240 seq.
Colebrooke on the Upanishads, *ibid.*, Vol. VIII, pp. 419 seq.

Ten years after the publication of the *L'Ezour Vedam* there appeared another anonymous work, the *Bagvadam* (Paris, 1788), less confused and more readable than its predecessor.

In marked contrast to the above two works, Sir Charles Wilkins made a fairly accurate translation of the *Bhagvat Geeta* published in London, 1785. It was enthusiastically received by the public both in England and France. Blake himself came under its spell for he did a drawing called 'The Bramins' showing Wilkins translating the Gita, no doubt seated cross-legged on the floor with the Bramins grouped around him in the traditional Indian manner. But this is pure conjecture for the drawing is lost and all we know about it is Blake's confession that he was told his costumes were wrong.[1]

In January 1788, a certain Col. Polier presented a copy of the Four Vedas, in the original Sanskrit, to Oxford University.[2] There seems to have been no English translation of the same, however, for eleven years later Dr. Priestley bemoans the fact.[3] Yet in 1786 Anquetil Duperron had already translated parts of the 'Oupnekhat' (Upanishads) which form an integral part of the Vedas.[4] He describes the text in his possession as being 478

[1] W. Blake, *A Descriptive Catalogue*, 1809, entry No. X, Geoffrey Keynes, *The Poetry and Prose of William Blake*, Nonesuch Press, one volume, third edition, London, 1932, p. 804. All references to this volume will be referred to as K. followed by the page number.

[2] Sir William Jones, Letter dated January 5, 1788, addressed to the Rev. Dr. Ford, Principal of Magdalen Hall, Oxford, introducing Col. Polier. *The Works of Sir W. Jones* with the Life of the Author by Lord Teignmouth, London, 1807, Vol. II, p. 133.

[3] Joseph Priestley, *A Comparison of the Institutions of Moses with those of the Hindoo and other antient Nations*, Northumberland, 1799, Introduction, pp. 1–2.

[4] Anquetil Duperron, 'Recherches historiques et geographiques sur l'Inde' in Jean Bernouilli's *Description historique et geographique de l'Inde*, Berlin, 1786, Tom. II, pp. 296–394.

pages in length and containing fifty 'oupnekhats', written in Persian with Sanskrit words intermixed.

The works of travellers, missionaries, historians, and critics, as well as translations proper from Indian religious and literary classics, were read and incorporated into their own writings by writers on folklore and mythology to prove their own peculiar theories. The passion for synthesizing and correlating the myths of various different nations is predominant in the works of Thomas Maurice, Jacob Bryant, Antoine Banier, Bernard Picart, Joseph Priestley, and Edward Davies, to mention only a few of the best known.[1] Thus Indian gods are identified with Assyrian, Egyptian, Greek, and Roman deities, the Bramins are considered the descendants of the ancient Druids, while the Biblical account of the origin and migration of races is twisted to fit in with eighteenth-century theories on the lost Atlantis and the belief that all races originated from Great Britain. In some measure, these views were also shared by Blake as Professor Denis Saurat long ago showed.[2]

Besides the sources already mentioned, there were two others from which knowledge of India came to Europe in Blake's day. Pictorial presentations of genuine Hindu statues, carvings, and pictures were not uncommon. The best known of such publications was Edward Moor's *Hindu Pantheon* (London, 1810).

[1] Thomas Maurice, *Indian Antiquities*, 7 vols. London, 1793–1800 Jacob Bryant, *A New System or an Analysis of Ancient Mythology*, London, 1774.

Antoine Banier, *Mythology and Fables of the Ancients explained from History*, London, 1734–40.

Bernard Picart, *The Ceremonies & Religious Customs of the various nations of the known World*, London, 1733.

Joseph Priestley, *A Comparison of the Institutions of Moses with those of the Hindoo and other antient Nations*, Northumberland, 1799. Edward Davies, *Celtic Researches*, London, 1804.

[2] Denis Saurat, *Blake and Modern Thought*, London, 1929.

Moor gives detailed descriptions of the important and little-known deities of the Hindu Pantheon, as well as a number of beautiful drawings of these gods and goddesses.

About the same time as John Johnson published Moor's *Hindu Pantheon*, Balthazar Solvyns brought out his fascinating volume, *Costumes of Hindostan*, (London, 1806), containing sixty coloured engravings with descriptions in English and French. It is more than likely that Blake knew both works well.

Lastly, there were private and public collections of Indian art treasures to which those interested could gain access. Moor himself acknowledges that several of his drawings in the *Hindu Pantheon* are copied from exhibits in the Museum at India House, London, and from the private collection of Colonel Stuart. No doubt other collections also existed, though it is very difficult to get authentic information regarding them today.

Even the cursory sketch given above of the various sources from which knowledge of India came to Europe in the eighteenth century reveals what a wealth of material was available to Blake if he chose to draw upon it. In keeping with the folklore writers and mythologists of his time, Blake's predominant interest is in Hindu philosophy and Hindu cosmogony, particularly where these concerned the Creation and the Fall of Man.

Hindu mythology contains various accounts of the Creation, and one of them is the myth describing the world as being spun from the bowels of a spider. This myth is alluded to by several of the mythologists mentioned above, and also impressed Blake's friend, Dr. Joseph Priestley, who writes,

> The production of all things from the substance of the Divine Being is thus represented by some of the Bramins. Comparing the First Cause to a spider, they say the universe

> was produced by that insect spinning out of its own entrails and belly; so that it brought forth first the elements, and then the celestial globes, etc., and that things are to continue in this state till the end of ages, when this spider will draw into its body the several threads which had issued from it, when all things will be destroyed and the world no longer exist, but as in the belly of the spider.[1]

With sardonic humour Blake uses this myth in his depiction of Urizen, the Intellect divorced from the Emotions (Luvah) and from the Imagination (Los), blind to the Divine Vision, cold, hard, coercive. In *The First Book of Urizen*, Blake describes this Zoa as wandering over the cities of his creation in 'pain and woe . . .'

> And wherever he wander'd, in sorrows
> Upon the aged heavens,
> A cold shadow follow'd behind him
> Like a spider's web, moist, cold & dim,
> Drawing out from his sorrowing soul.[2]

In *Vala* or *The Four Zoas*, Blake is even more explicit. The children of Urizen's creation accuse him, crying,

> O Spider, spread thy web! Enlarge thy bones & fill'd
> With marrow, sinews & flesh, Exalt thyself, attain a voice.
> Call to thy dark arm'd hosts; for all the sons of Men muster together
> To desolate their cities: Man shall be no more![3]

[1] Joseph Priestley, *op. cit.*, p. 50.
[2] W. Blake, *The First Book of Urizen*, 1794, Chap. VIII, v. 6; K. 257.
[3] W. Blake, *Vala or The Four Zoas*, 1795–1804, Night I, 397–400, K. 294.

In Night VI of *Vala* the web is described as woven from Urizen's 'mantle of years' and stretching from 'Vortex to Vortex' of his heavens. When Urizen is faced by the revolt of his creation he runs back 'into his dire Web, scattering fleecy snows'.

As he ascended, howling loud, the Web vibrated strong,
From heaven to heaven, from globe to globe. . . .
Slow roll the massy Globes at his command & slow o'erwheel
The dismal squadrons of Urthona weaving the dire Web
In their progressions, & preparing Urizen's path before him.[1]

An illustration from an early prophetic work, *Europe*, shows plainly the spider and its web entangling Man and Nature in its meshes.[2]

Blake has borrowed the main elements of the Hindu creation myth. The 'celestial globes', mentioned by Dr. Priestley, duly appear in the passages quoted above; so do the 'several threads' spun out of the spider's entrails and belly. Finally, there is the association of the spider with the destruction of all things. But here the resemblance ends. In his definition of the web, and in his development of the character of Urizen, Blake is entirely original. He defines the web as 'The Net of Religion' having twisted cords and knotted meshes 'twisted like to the human brain'.[2] As for Urizen, he is not only the spider of the Hindu creation myth spinning out 'vast enormities' from himself, but a great deal else. By using the framework of the Hindu myth Blake emphasizes an essential aspect of Urizen's character. The double allusion, to the myth on the one hand, and to man's

[1] Ibid. Night VI, conclusion, K. 365.

[2] W. Blake, *Europe, a Prophecy*, 1794, pl. 12. B.M. copy.

Reason on the other, would have been obvious to a contemporary reader but it is apt to be overlooked today.

Turning to other Hindu creation myths familiar to eighteenth-century readers, we find two entirely different accounts of the Creation given in the Dissertation prefixed to Alexander Dow's *History of Hindostan*. In the first account, Dow, quoting from the *Bedang Shaster*, translates a dialogue between Brimha, the Wisdom of God, and Narud, Reason, the son of Brimha. Narud asks, 'How did God create the world?' Brimha replies:

> Affection dwelt with God from all eternity. It was of three different kinds, the creative, the preserving and the destructive. The first is represented by Brimha, the second by Bishen, and the third by Shibah. . . . The affection of God then produced power, and power at a proper conjunction of time and fate, embraced goodness, and produced matter. The three qualities then acting upon matter, produced the universe in the following manner. From the opposite actions of the creative and destructive quality in matter, self-motion first arose. Self-motion was of three kinds; the first inclining to plasticity, the second to discord, and the third to rest. The discordant actions then produced Akash, which invisible element possessed the quality of conveying sound; it produced air a palpable element; fire, a visible element; water, a fluid element; and earth, a solid element.
>
> The Akash dispersed itself abroad, Air formed the atmosphere; fire, collecting itself, blazed forth in the host of heaven; water rose to the surface of the earth, being forced from beneath by the gravity of the latter element. Thus broke forth the world from the veil of darkness in which it was formerly comprehended by God. Order rose over the

universe. The seven heavens were formed, and the seven worlds were fixed in their places; there to remain till the great dissolution, when all things shall be absorbed into God.

God seeing the earth in full bloom, and that vegetation was strong from its seeds, called forth for the first time, Intellect, which he endued with various organs and shapes, to form a diversity of animals upon the earth. He endued animals with five senses, feeling, seeing, smelling, tasting and hearing. But to man he gave reflexion to raise him above the beasts of the field.

The creatures were created male and female that they might propagate their species upon the earth. Every herb bore the seed of its kind, that the world might be clothed with verdure, and all animals provided with food.[1]

There are several points of resemblance between Blake and this account of the Creation. For instance, Blake is in complete agreement with the Hindu conception of *Samsara*, mundane existence, which consists of discordant elements in opposition to one another. This belief is further developed in the *Bhagvat Gita*. Blake, writing in *The Marriage of Heaven and Hell*, states:

Without Contraries is no progression. Attraction and Repulsion, Reason and Energy, Love and Hate, are necessary to Human existence.[2]

In the above quotation Blake uses the word, 'progression' in the same sense as 'self-motion' of the *Bedang Shaster* quoted by

[1] Alexander Dow, *History of Hindostan*, 2 vols. London, 1768, Vol. I, pp. xl–xlii.

[2] W. Blake, *The Marriage of Heaven and Hell*, 1793, pl. 3; K. 191.

Dow. Self-motion is said to be of three kinds, 'the first inclining to plasticity, the second to discord, and the third to rest'. Blake also adopts these categories for his worlds of Eden, Ulro, and Beulah respectively. The Eternals dwell in Eden where their senses expand and contract at will expressing plasticity as described in the *Bedang Shaster*. In Ulro, on the other hand, Blake's symbol for the Land of Error and of this 'vegetable universe' characterized by generation and death, discord is rife. Blake devotes the whole of the long poem, *Vala or The Four Zoas*, to describing the 'fortuitous concourse of incoherent/ Discordant principles of Love & Hate'.[1] Whereas plasticity and discord are found in Eden and Ulro, rest and repose are typical of Beulah, a state of harmony where the intellect and the emotions are at peace and united as in a happy marriage which is what the word 'Beulah' means.[2]

As one would expect, Blake does not borrow any of the three aspects of the Hindu Trinity, Creator, Preserver, Destroyer, but uses specifically Christian categories, Creation, Redemption, and Judgment, in showing how Ulro, the Land of Error, can be redeemed by Christ.

The Hindu belief that Intellect was 'endued with various organs and shapes to form a diversity of animals upon the earth', is distorted by Blake to depict his own vision of Urizen's loathly creation:

> And his world teem'd vast enormities,
> Fright'ning, faithless, fawning
> Portions of life, similitudes

[1] *Vala*, Night II, lines 102, 103; K. 306.

[2] Beulah occurs in Bunyan's *Pilgrim's Progress* where it means married bliss. See D. J. Sloss & J. P. R. Wallis, *The Prophetic Writings of William Blake*, Oxford, 1926, Vol. II, Index, entry on Beulah.

> Of a foot, or a hand, or a head,
> Or an heart, or an eye; they swam mischevous,
> Dread terrors, delighting in blood.[1]

One by one, Blake describes these noisome creatures. First Thiriel 'like a man from a cloud born'; next Utha, emerges from the waters lamenting loudly. He is followed by Grodna rending 'the deep earth, howling amaz'd', and finally, Fuzon, flames out.

> All his Eternal sons in like manner;
> His daughters from green herbs & cattle,
> From monsters & worms of the pit.[2]

Unlike the Intellect power of the *Bedang Shaster*, Blake's Urizen is aware that his creation groans under the weight of his oppressive laws.

The second account of the Creation given by Dow in his *History of Hindostan* is very different from the first, and shows further resemblances between Blake and Hindu cosmogony. A full quotation from Dow will make this clear.

> Brimha existed from all eternity, in a form of infinite dimensions. When it pleased him to create the world, he said, 'Rise up, O Brimha'. Immediately a spirit of the colour of flame issued from his navel, having four heads and four hands. Brimha gazing round, and seeing nothing but the immense image, out of which he had proceeded, he travelled a thousand years, to endeavour to comprehend its dimensions.

[1] W. Blake, *The First Book of Urizen*, Chap. VIII, v. 2. K. 256.
[2] *Ibid.*, Chap. VIII, v. 3. K. 256.

But after all his toil, he found himself as much at a loss as before.

Lost in amazement, Brimha gave over his journey. He fell prostrate and praised what he saw, with his four mouths. The Almighty then with a voice like ten thousand thunders, was pleased to say: Thou hast done well, O Brimha, for thou canst not comprehend me! Go and create the world—How can I create it?—Ask of me and power shall be given unto thee—O God, said Brimha, thou art almighty in power!

Brimha forthwith perceived the idea of things as if floating before his eyes. He said LET THEM BE, and all that he saw became real before him. Then fear struck the frame of Brimha, lest those things should be annihilated. O immortal Brimha! he cried, who shall preserve those things which I behold. In the instant a spirit of a blue colour issued from Brimha's mouth, and said aloud, I WILL. Then shall thy name be Bishen (Providence of God), because thou hast undertaken to preserve all things.

Brimha then commanded Bishen to go and create all animals, with vegetables for their substance, to possess that earth which he himself had made. Bishen forthwith created all manner of beasts, fish, fowl, insects and reptiles. Trees and grass rose also beneath his hands, for Brimha had invested him with power. But man was still wanting to rule the whole: and Brimha commanded Bishen to form him. Bishen began the work but the men he made were idiots with great bellies, for he could not inspire them with knowledge; so that in everything but in shape they resembled the beasts of the field. They had no passion but to satisfy their carnal appetites.

Brimha, offended at the men, destroyed them, and produced four persons from his own breath, whom he called by four different names. The name of the first was SINNOC (Body), of the second, SINNUNDA (Life) of the third, SONNATIN (Permanency), and of the fourth SONNIN-KUNAR (Intellectual existence). These four persons were ordered by Brimha to rule over the creatures and to possess for ever the world. But they refused to do anything but praise God, having nothing of the destructive quality in their composition.

Brimha, for this contempt of his orders, became angry, and lo! a brown spirit started from between his eyes. He sat down before Brimha and began to weep: Then lifting up his eyes he asked him, 'Who am I, and where shall be the place of my abode?' Thy name shall be Rudder (Weeper) said Brimha, and all nature shall be the place of thine abode. But rise up, O Rudder, and form man to govern the world.

Rudder immediately obeyed the orders of Brimha. He began to work, but the men he made were fiercer than tigers, having nothing but the destructive qualities in their composition. They, however, soon destroyed one another, for anger was their only passion. Brimha, Bishen and Rudder then joined their different powers. They created ten men whose names were Narud (Reason), Dico (Ingenuity), Bashista (Emulation), Birga (Humility), Kirku (Piety), Pulla (Pride), Pulista (Patience), Ongira (Charity), Otteri (Deceit), and Murichi (Mortality): the general appellation of the whole was the Munies (the Inspired). Brimha then produced Dirmo (Fortune) from his breast, Adirmo (Misfortune) from his back, Loab (Appetite) from his lip, and Kam (Love) from his heart. This last being a beautiful female, Brimha looked upon her with amorous eyes. But the

Munies told him, that she was his own daughter; upon which he shrunk back, and produced a blushing virgin Ludja (Shame). Brimha thinking his body defiled by throwing his eyes upon Kam, changed it and produced ten women, one of which was given to each of the Munies.

From their union mankind was propagated.[1]

Many points of resemblance emerge between Blake and the above account of the Creation. Just as Brihma, the uncreated, unmanifested God, creates his manifest Self, also called Brimha, who, failing to understand from whence he proceeded and for what purpose, falls prostrate before his own image in idolatrous worship, even so, Blake's Albion falls prostrate before his own shadow.

> Then Albion ascended mourning into the porches of his Palace,
> Above him rose a Shadow from his wearied intellect,
> Of living gold, pure, perfect, holy; in white linen pure he hover'd,
> A sweet entrancing self-delusion, a wat'ry vision of Albion, . .
>
> Albion fell upon his face prostrate before the wat'ry Shadow,
> Saying: 'O Lord, whence is this change? thou knowest I am nothing!' . . .
>
> O I am nothing when I enter into judgment with thee!
> If thou withdraw thy breath, I die & vanish into Hades;[2]

[1] Dow, *op. cit.*, Vol. I, pp. xlvi–xlix.

[2] W. Blake, *Jerusalem, the Emanation of the Giant Albion, 1804–1820*, pl. 29; K. 603.

Again, there is a certain resemblance between Bishen of the *Bedang Shaster* and Blake's Urizen. Bishen is ordered by Brimha to create Man to rule the world, but the men he creates are 'idiots with great bellies, for he could not inspire them with knowledge; so that in everything but in shape they resembled the beasts of the field. They had no passion but to satisfy their carnal appetites'. Urizen, although he is Intellect, he is intellect divorced from the Imagination so that his creatures bear only a 'similitude' to Man, being in every other way creatures of appetite like the men created by Bishen. Just as Brimha destroys Bishen's men so Urizen's creation is also doomed to destruction by its very nature.

Another striking resemblance can be noticed between the 'four persons' produced from Brimha's breath, and the four Zoas of Blake. Brimha's four persons are: Sinnoc the Body; Sinnunda, Life; Sonnatin, Permanency; and Sonninkunar, Intellectual existence. Blake's four Zoas are: Tharmas the Body; Luvah, Emotions; Urizen, Intellect; and Los-Urthona, the Imagination and the Spirit. The four persons of the *Bedang Shaster* together seem to represent a living body of permanent intellectual existence. This would form an apt description of Blake's Four Zoas in their primal unity when they dwelt in Eden, Blake's term for a state of keen intellectual activity. Before their fall into separation, and after their re-union described in *Jerusalem*, Blake's Four Zoas behave in exactly the same way as the four persons of the *Bedang Shaster*, 'refusing to do anything but to praise God'.

The resemblance between Blake's Zoas and the four persons of the *Bedang Shaster*, however, must not be strained too far, for, as has been said already, Blake is essentially a Christian visionary and his Zoas are more akin to the Zoas or Living Creatures of Ezekiel's vision than to anything else.

The birth of beings from various parts of the human body is found in the second account of the Creation given by Dow and also in Blake. Just as Brimha produces Fortune from his breast, Misfortune from his back, Appetite from his lip, and Love from his heart, so in Blake's writings beings are born from the bosom, the back, the loins, the nostrils, the hair, the brain, the feet, the heart, the head, the breath and the throat.[1]

Blake, however, is deliberately inconsistent in the parentage he bestows upon his symbols. Thus, Satan is born from the 'Hermaphroditic bosom' of 'Congregated assemblies of wicked men' [2] and also tears his way from Albion's loins.[3] Luvah rends his way in thunder and smoke from Enitharmon's heart,[4] and also from her loins,[5] as well as the loins of Albion.[6] In one place the Twelve Sons of Albion emerge from his bosom [7] and in another from the throat of Hand.[8] The Spectre, or the cruel rationalizing power, is usually born from the back,[9] but the Spectre of Urthona springs from the 'breathing Nostrils Of Enion',[10] and his 'masculine spirit' from Enion's brain.[11] The Spectre of Tharmas, on the other hand, issues from his feet 'in flames of fire'.[12] The 'spectrous dead' are 'breath'd forth upon the wind', with 'sighs of love', by Enitharmon,[13] while she herself and Urthona are born from 'Albion's dark'ning locks'.[14]

[1] Beings born from the bosom: K. 233–4; 300, 408, 483, 583, 587, 605, 611, 641, 711; from the back: K. 468, 556, 611; from the loins: K. 253–254; 296, 333, 377, 598, 611, 639; from the nostrils: K. 333; from the hair: K. 603; from the brain: K. 377, 603; from the feet: K. 280; from the heart: K. 343, 348, 378; from the head: K. 366; from the breath: 384, 385, 399, 400, 405, 413; from the throat: K. 690.

[2] K. 408. [3] K. 598. [4] K. 343. [5] K. 296. [6] K. 639. [7] K. 611. [8] K. 690. [9] K. 468, 556, 581, 611. [10] K. 333. [11] K. 377. [12] K. 280. [13] K. 384. [14] K. 603.

Blake is justified in this complex manipulation of the births, deaths, and rebirths of his characters in the Prophetic Books for, as E. J. Ellis points out, Revolution (Orc) has more than one cause, and so has Passion (Luvah) to mention only two important Blakean symbols.[1]

Enough has now been said to show what use Blake made of some of the popular Hindu creation myths of his times. In each of the three myths discussed, Blake adopts the framework of the original and infuses his own subtle thought into it. Yet a knowledge of that framework is essential if the force of his own message is to be fully appreciated. He is concerned only with the Eternal as it is revealed here and now in earthly life. In his *Vision of the Last Judgment* he writes:

> The Nature of Visionary Fancy, or Imagination, is very little known, & the Eternal nature & permanence of its ever Existent Images is consider'd as less permanent than the things of Vegetative & Generative Nature; yet the Oak dies as well as the Lettuce, but Its Eternal Image & Individuality never dies, but renews by its seed; just so the Imaginative Image returns by the seed of Contemplative Thought.[2]
>
> If the Spectator could enter into these Images in his Imagination, approaching them on the Fiery Chariot of his Contemplative Thought, if he could Enter into Noah's Rainbow or into his bosom, or could make a Friend & Companion of one of these Images of wonder, which always intreats him to leave mortal things (as he must know), then

[1] E. J. Ellis, *The Real Blake*, London, 1907, chap. entitled 'The Real Blake'.

[2] W. Blake, *A Vision of the Last Judgment*, 1810, pp. 68–9. K. 829.

would he arise from his Grave, then would he meet the Lord in the Air & then he would be happy.[1]

The poet and seer in Blake dominate the facts of mundane existence. Through the visual image and the written word is heard the clear voice of the prophet 'calling the lapsed soul' to cast off Error and embrace the Truth. Whether Blake's imagination deals with the sordid or the sublime, his aim is single, his vision pure. Herein lies his greatness and his intrinsic worth.

O search & see: turn your eyes upward: open, O thou World Of Love & Harmony in Man: expand thy ever lovely Gates![2]

[1] *Ibid.* pp. 82–4. K. 836.
[2] W. Blake, *Jerusalem*, chap. II, p. 44. K. 636.

VII

She Shall be Called Woman

by

Piloo Nanavutty

(India)

VII

She Shall be Called Woman

AMONG THE SMALL but interesting number of drawings by Blake in the Print Room of the Metropolitan Museum of Art, New York, there is a little known and undated water-colour inscribed, in large, bold lettering, 'She shall be called Woman'.

It was formerly in the Butts Collection, and is No. 106 in Rossetti's annotated lists of Blake's pictures, appended to Gilchrist's *Life of William Blake*, where it is given the title, 'The Creation of Eve—"She shall be called Woman" '.

It appears to be a companion piece to 'The Angel of the Divine Presence clothing Adam and Eve with coats of skin' (1803), a water colour formerly in the collection of the late Mr. W. Graham Robertson, and for many years now in the Fitzwilliam Museum, Cambridge.[1]

On comparing the two drawings under discussion, one is struck by the general similarity in style and colouring, and by the close resemblance between the patriarchal figures of the Angels and their features. It is, therefore, not unreasonable to suppose that the undated design at the Metropolitan Museum of Art was executed about the same time as the drawing in the Fitzwilliam Museum, that is, *circa* 1803, possibly a little earlier, as, chronologically, the Creation of Eve precedes the Fall.

A careful examination of the drawing at the Metropolitan Museum of Art reveals symbolic details which explain the

[1] Darrell Figgis, *The Paintings of William Blake*, London, 1925, pl. 2.

significance of the whole. Blake is illustrating the well-known verses:

> And the Lord God caused a deep sleep to fall upon Adam, and he slept: and he took one of his ribs, and closed up the flesh instead thereof;
>
> And the rib which the Lord God had taken from the man, made he a woman, and brought her unto the man.
>
> And Adam said, This is now bone of my bones, and flesh of my flesh: she shall be called Woman, because she was taken out of Man.[1]

In the foreground of the picture at the Metropolitan Museum of Art, the naked Adam, half risen from sleep, reclines upon an oak leaf. Blake associated this leaf with the pangs of birth and human misery as well as with the cruel sacrifices carried out by the Druids in dark oak groves at dead of night.[2] In *Jerusalem*: 59, he refers to the 'Oak of Weeping' and the 'Palm of Suffering'. The significance of the symbol is apparent in the frontispiece to his own emblematical work, *The Gates of Paradise* (1793), where a chrysalis, with an infant's head emerging from it, lies on an oak leaf, while a caterpillar crawls upon another. An apposite couplet explains the emblem:

> The Caterpiller on the Leaf
> Reminds thee of thy Mother's Grief.

Again, the oak leaf appears in a drawing for the Creation of Eve, viz. design 6 of the water colour illustrations for the

[1] *Genesis*, 2. vv. 21–23.

[2] See D. J. Sloss & J. P. R. Wallis, *The Prophetic Writings of William Blake*, Oxford, 1926, Vol. II, Index, Druid, Druidism, pp. 148–151.

'The Angel of the Divine Presence clothing Adam and Eve with Coats of Skin'
Water colour by William Blake
(Courtesy of the Fitzwilliam Museum, Cambridge)

'She Shall Be Called Woman'
Water colour by William Blake
(*Courtesy of the Metropolitan Museum of Art, New York*)

Paradise Lost Series (1808), which shows Adam, in deep sleep, lying upon a large oak leaf, still recognizable under its decorative flourishes. The hated oak groves are prominently placed in the middle distance.[1]

Turning back to the water colour at the Metropolitan Museum of Art, it will be seen that the Angel of the Divine Presence is the central figure in the composition. He holds Adam's right hand in his right, while he leads Eve forward, holding her right hand in his left. His clinging draperies, tinted a shell pink, swirl round his feet as he gently floats to earth. Eve is naked, with a profusion of golden red hair which falls in alluring waves down her back and shoulders. She looks with grave wonder at Adam who returns her gaze in wide-eyed and open mouthed astonishment.

Eve, being a woman, steps forward with her left foot to emphasize the physical side of her nature.[2] She descends from a cloud-bank coloured a bright cobalt blue. Behind her rise other clouds painted pink and white.

Oddly enough, Adam's locks are also a bright blue. This is not as curious as it appears at first sight. Blake uses the pictorial image of the cloud to represent confusion of mind and petty worries. He speaks symbolically of 'Cloudy Doubts & Reasoning Cares'.[3] In the present instance he would seem to imply that the woman always brings in her train worries and cares which enter man's head and dominate his intellect to the exclusion of all else. Blake resented the control of man's mental and emotional life by the 'female Will', which he

[1] Figgis, *op. cit.*, pl. 19.

[2] See Joseph H. Wicksteed, *Blake's Vision of the Book of Job*, London, 1924, Appendix B.

[3] Blake, *The Gates of Paradise*, emblem no. 4, caption.

looked upon as intrinsically evil and possessive. Hence the significance of Adam's locks being the same colour as the cloud on which Eve stands.

Beneath the cloud, Blake has drawn four sheep grazing. Close beside them, on the extreme right, is the profile of a lion's face, comically human. He has curling locks, a closed eye with long lashes, and a marked smirk upon his lips.[1] To be sure, the lion and the lamb lie down together in Paradise, but the amused expression on the lion's features seems to indicate that Adam's domestic bliss will be short-lived.

On the left margin is a bare tree with a luscious vine tendril creeping up its branches. Clusters of purple grapes, symbolizing carnal ecstasy, hang from it. Two gaudy plumaged cockatoos are seated upon the vine. Like the grand ladies of society, they seem to be indulging in vociferous approbation of the scene depicted beneath them. Their behaviour is in keeping with Adam's vulgar amazement.

In the middle distance a flock of sheep are grazing. Beyond them, is a stream flowing past woods and low hills. In contrast to the purple of the grapes, and the red, green, orange, and violet in the plumage of the cockatoos, Blake has used subdued tones of grey-greens, fawn, and beige to depict the pastoral serenity of the landscape in the background of the picture. This is offset by the flaming red of a new dawn rising towards the left. Following the highlights of the drawing, the eye travels from the red-gold tints of Eve's hair to the cobalt blue of the cloud she stands on, past the startling colour of Adam's

[1] Cf. the lions passed by Christian in Bunyan's *The Pilgrim's Progress*, illustrated with 29 water colour drawings by William Blake, printed at the Spiral Press, New York, for members of the Limited Editions Club, 1941, pl. XVIII. The original drawings are in the Frick Collection, New York.

locks to the gay purple of the grape clusters and the vivid plumage of the cockatoos.

The satiric touches in the design recall the lines in *Jerusalem* : 56,

> What may Man be? who can tell! But what may Woman be
> To have power over Man from Cradle to corruptible
> Grave?

Although these words were not engraved to illustrate this particular drawing, they throw light on the mood in which Blake conceived and executed his theme.

VIII

Blake's Drawings for Young's Night Thoughts

by

H. M. Margoliouth
Oriel College, Oxford (*Great Britain*)

VIII

Blake's Drawings for Young's Night Thoughts

Of all Blake's work his water-coloured drawings for Young's *Night Thoughts* must be the least known in comparison with their quantity and importance. Yet they must have been his main occupation for about eighteen months, from the autumn of 1795 to the spring of 1797. From then until 1874 they were unknown. The facts are set out by Sir Geoffrey Keynes in *Blake Studies* (1949), pp. 56–66. In June 1875 J. Comyns Carr devoted to these drawings seven pages (728–735) of an article on Blake in the *Cornhill*. For the second edition (1880) of Gilchrist's *Life of Blake* F. Shields wrote an appendix (vol. ii, pp. 289–307) describing some of the drawings in detail, but it was not included in Graham Robertson's reprint of the first edition (1906, 1922, 1928). Sir Geoffrey Keynes described thirty of them in 1927. There is very little else to read about them. Those thirty drawings were reproduced (five in colour) by the Harvard University Press (1927), Wright's *Life of William Blake* (1929) reproduced six, four of them new, and Keynes's *Blake Studies* (1949) five, three of them new. That makes thirty-seven out of 537, and in addition there are, of course, the forty-three engraved by Blake for Edwards's June 1797 publication of the first four Nights. Thus 457 are unknown except to those who have seen the originals, which have since 1929 been, by American generosity, in the Print Room of the British Museum.

That 1797 publication is not easily obtainable. The first two Nights have been reproduced (Butterworth, 1911), Soupault's

William Blake (1928) reproduced fourteen of the engravings and some have been reproduced elsewhere. Binyon's *Engraved Designs of William Blake* (1926) catalogues all forty-three, quoting the line asterisked on each page as being the subject of the picture and also quoting the short descriptions, most certainly not written by Blake, which accompanied the 1797 publication. Binyon also reproduced the engraved title-page to Night III. A few of the engravings may not have been reproduced at all. In any case reproduction of the engravings is not the same thing as reproduction of the drawings. Most of them lost much by losing the colours. Moreover, Blake's engraving in 1796–1797 had not reached the mastery of the *Job* period. There is, for example, too much conventional line and criss-cross work in the backgrounds. Some of the drawings are reversed in the engravings. In some of the engravings the design has been altered a little from the drawing. Interesting examples are provided by the engravings for page 37 (Night II, p. 35, lines 563–580 in the drawings) and page 63 (Night III, p. 33, lines 511–528 in the drawings).

In the first of these the asterisked line, in both engraving and drawing, is

Love, and Love only, is the Loan for Love.

To illustrate this Blake chose the story of the Good Samaritan. He has got at the heart of Young's line. The injured man is not just a lay figure. He lies on his back with his head raised in horror, and his right hand makes a determined gesture of refusal. The Good Samaritan faces him and holds a closed egg-shaped vessel decorated on the outside with a serpent in relief. The injured man is a good Jew. He is horrified at being rescued by a

Samaritan, whose vessel of healing oil or wine seems as sinister as a serpent. Blake had not yet coined the phrase about corporeal friends being spiritual enemies, but here is an apparent example of it—unless indeed the injured man fears that the Samaritan may be a corporeal enemy also. Perhaps finishing you off with poison is just what a Samaritan would do. The Good Samaritan persists. He hopes by lending love to be repaid with love. At any rate love is the only loan which can be so repaid.

The trees in the engraving differ considerably from those in the drawing. In both there is a coverlet over the lower part of the injured man, but in the engraving it is over his feet too, whereas in the drawing they project from the blue coverlet. But the most interesting difference is in the face of the Good Samaritan. In the drawing his mouth is a little more open and his head more bent than in the engraving: he looks shocked or at least perplexed, whereas in the engraving he looks more sure of himself and, perhaps, more beneficent.

On p. 63 of the engraved edition the asterisked line is

This KING OF TERRORS is the PRINCE OF PEACE.

It is the last page of Night III. Edwards was responsible for the capitals and also for a complete change from Blake's intention.

It must be explained that the pages of text, round which and in connexion with which Blake made his drawings, contain on an average less than twenty lines. Edwards provided an engraving for less than half his pages; a full page with an engraving usually contains thirty lines and one without an engraving also thirty, the wide margins remaining blank. Consequently the lines on an engraved page can only partly correspond to those on a page of the drawings. It is, however, only on p. 63 that Edwards made a real, and doubtless deliberate, muddle.

On p. 33 (lines 511–528), the *last but one* of Night III, Blake asterisked

Death, the Great Counsellor, who Man inspires.

He then drew a white-bearded, half-reclining figure of Death, holding an open scroll between his hands. The scroll has on it a few indeterminate marks to indicate writing. The 'Great Counsellor' looks straight in front of him, wise and beneficent.

On p. 34 (lines 529–544), the last of Night III, Blake asterisked

Spring from our Fetters; fasten in the Skies.

The picture shows Death removing a chain from the left ankle of a man who is preparing to rise and already lifts his left arm to the sky. On the left a woman rises, with both arms outstretched, into the blue sky.

Edwards did not include this drawing. He preferred to end the Night with the more striking picture of Death, but the line about the Great Counsellor was back on his previous page (62). So a new line, the last but two, was asterisked, and also heavily capitalized, when the lines were printed in the blank space left by the engraving: but the reason for the scroll, which should have contained counsel, is no longer apparent. In fact the whole picture is attached to the wrong line.

There is one change from the drawing. The indeterminate marks on the scroll are replaced by nine short lines of Hebrew lettering, but it is very queer Hebrew. In the first place it is reversed. Blake evidently engraved it from right to left on the

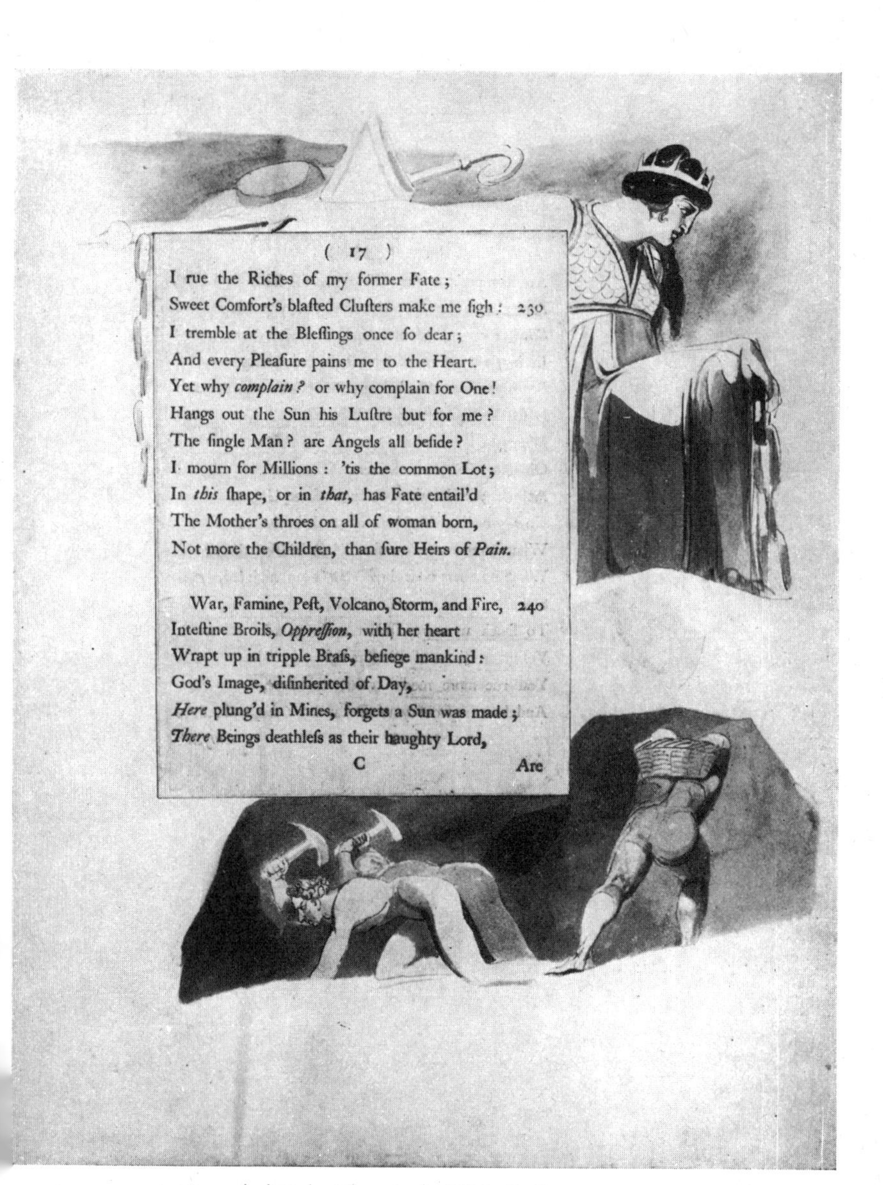
(17)

I rue the Riches of my former Fate;
Sweet Comfort's blaſted Cluſters make me ſigh: 230
I tremble at the Bleſſings once ſo dear;
And every Pleaſure pains me to the Heart.
Yet why *complain?* or why complain for One!
Hangs out the Sun his Luſtre but for me?
The ſingle Man? are Angels all beſide?
I mourn for Millions: 'tis the common Lot;
In *this* ſhape, or in *that*, has Fate entail'd
The Mother's throes on all of woman born,
Not more the Children, than ſure Heirs of *Pain*.

War, Famine, Peſt, Volcano, Storm, and Fire, 240
Inteſtine Broils, *Oppreſſion*, with her heart
Wrapt up in tripple Braſs, beſiege mankind:
God's Image, diſinherited of Day,
Here plung'd in Mines, forgets a Sun was made;
There Beings deathleſs as their haughty Lord,

C Are

Young's 'Night Thoughts': Night I, lines 229–245
Drawing by William Blake
(*Courtesy of The British Museum*)

Young's 'Night Thoughts': Night VIII, lines 1309–1317
Drawing by William Blake
(*Courtesy of The British Museum*)

plate with the result that a mirror-image, from left to right, appears on the page. A first impression, however, that it is a meaningless jumble of letters has to be partly modified, because Blake has almost certainly confused letters of similar but not identical form. A Hebraist tells me that reasonable guesses at what Blake meant to write may reveal words meaning 'thou' (twice), 'death', 'the fire' (twice), and 'dust', though a good deal must remain completely unintelligible. In another of these drawings (ix, p. 17, lines 314–334) there are two Hebrew words, meaning 'hereafter pain' and referring to 'Awful Eternity! offended Queen!', which are fairly correct. There is also some Hebrew lettering in Night V, p. 25 (the Sibyl), but it was at some later date that Blake learnt enough Hebrew to be accurate in the Enoch, Laocoön, and Job pictures. Here he seems to have been provided with some Hebrew, perhaps not very legible, of which he made a muddle. It does look, however, as if perhaps an effort was made to adapt the counsel to the 'King of Terrors'—not a very successful adaptation.

To work right through the 537 drawings is a fascinating task; to read right through Young's *Night Thoughts* is less fascinating, but it is not as wearisome as we are sometimes led to expect. I am sure of one thing: Blake did not despise his author. He did not asterisk lines in the first Night before making the drawings, but after that he generally, not always, did so, and he also sometimes marked or underlined other lines that struck him. The otherworldliness of Young's poem, its insistence on immortality and the values which a firm belief in immortality compels, must have appealed to him strongly. At least twice he remembered Young's actual words years later. Young's Night VI, line 655 runs

Of two eternities amazing Lord!

The two eternities are separated by the Creation. The reminiscence of Young may help to explain what was in Blake's mind when he wrote (*Milton* 14; 11 in Sloss and Wallis):

> The Sin was begun in Eternity, and will not rest to Eternity,
> Till two Eternitys meet together,

or, twice in *Jerusalem* (86 and 98), 'from Eternity to Eternity'.

About twenty-one years after finishing his drawings for the *Night Thoughts* Blake reissued his 1793 *Gates of Paradise* with new verses which include the well-known Epilogue beginning:

> Truly, My Satan, thou art but a Dunce.

That 'Truly' is an endorsement of the last line of Young's Night VIII,

> Thy Master, *Satan*, I dare call a dunce.

Blake had not asterisked the line, but his drawing shows Satan, red-skinned, bald with white tufts, wearing only a blue skirt, kneeling and bowing to Christ, and offering him a stone to be made bread. Christ, upright in white, holds up his left hand in refusal. Satan knew no better!

Much more important is the fact that some of these drawings have value not only in themselves or as helping us to know Blake's mind during these eighteen months from which we have no poetry, but also because they reappear with some changes in later or greater pictures. Sir Geoffrey Keynes reproduced ix, p. 19, illustrating 'those Shouts of Joy, that shake the whole *Ethereal*', the line of praising angels whose raised arms cross each other and suggest an unending host, the picture which we all know in its most developed form in *Job*, Illustration xiv, 'When the morning Stars sang together'. But there are others. On Night I, p. 6, which has no asterisked line, is a drawing which was not engraved. The main figure is of the back view of a naked traveller. He has a stick in his left hand, his right arm is bent over his head, the right leg which is in front is bent, and his left foot far behind (so many of Blake's figures take immense strides) is raised on the toes. There are also three children, one reading and two playing, and a large tomb of which no one takes any notice. The main figure is, except in two points, exactly the same as the main figure on plate 97 of *Jerusalem*, the climax of Albion's travailing and travelling, where, standing on the dark-green edge of Earth, disregarding the waning moon and single star to his right, he [1] looks under his raised right arm straight into the great sunrays. Instead of the walking-stick his left hand now holds the globe of light, the sun from which the vast rays stream. It is a notable development. The other difference, a suggestion of clothing about the thigh, seems unimportant.

The same change, globe of light for walking-stick, is found in the well-known frontispiece to *Jerusalem*. In Night II, p. 28, another unengraved drawing, the asterisk is against

The cunning Fugitive is swift by stealth.

The fugitive is life. As sometimes happens, it is here not the actual line but the whole passage which Blake illustrates. A man is entering the house of Death. We see the back of a young-looking traveller with round hat, sleeved long coat, legs

[1] Or Los, but these distinctions fade with the final integration.

bare from the knees, stick in right hand, whose left foot is *on* the threshold and whose right foot is half lifted. His left hand is spread out. A white-bearded man has half-opened the Gothic door in a church-like building.

In the frontispiece to *Jerusalem* we have the same figure, who in his right hand holds not a walking-stick but a globe of light. It is his right foot that is *over* the threshold, for by this time Blake had come to symbolize spiritual and material by right and left respectively. Death no longer appears, nor do some minor figures and decorations. In fact, though the man is the same, the picture no longer represents the approach to physical death but the voluntary entering by the imagination of that grave of the spirit in which Man lies and from which he must be redeemed. That was part of Blake's developed Christianity. One cannot say when precisely the *Jerusalem* picture was made, but its engraving was more than twenty years after the *Night Thoughts* illustrations.

The correspondence between the main figures in each of these pairs of pictures is too close to be explained by visual memory, even when we allow for Blake's exceptional powers of visualization. He must have had copies of the drawings, or preliminary sketches for them, by him.[1] He cannot have had the drawings we now possess. They were the property of the publisher Edwards, who had paid for them (twenty guineas only, if the story is true) and in whose family they remained for some eighty years. In both these pairs of pictures there is a traveller; and a traveller, not necessarily a pilgrim, figures frequently in these drawings in many different attitudes, situa-

[1] Keynes, *Pencil Drawings by William Blake* (1927), reproduces a sketch of the *Night Thoughts*, i. 6 and *Jerusalem* 97 figure. He is reversed (stick in right hand) and climbs a steep valley.

Young's 'Night Thoughts': Night IX, lines 1865–1885
Drawing by William Blake
(*Courtesy of The British Museum*)

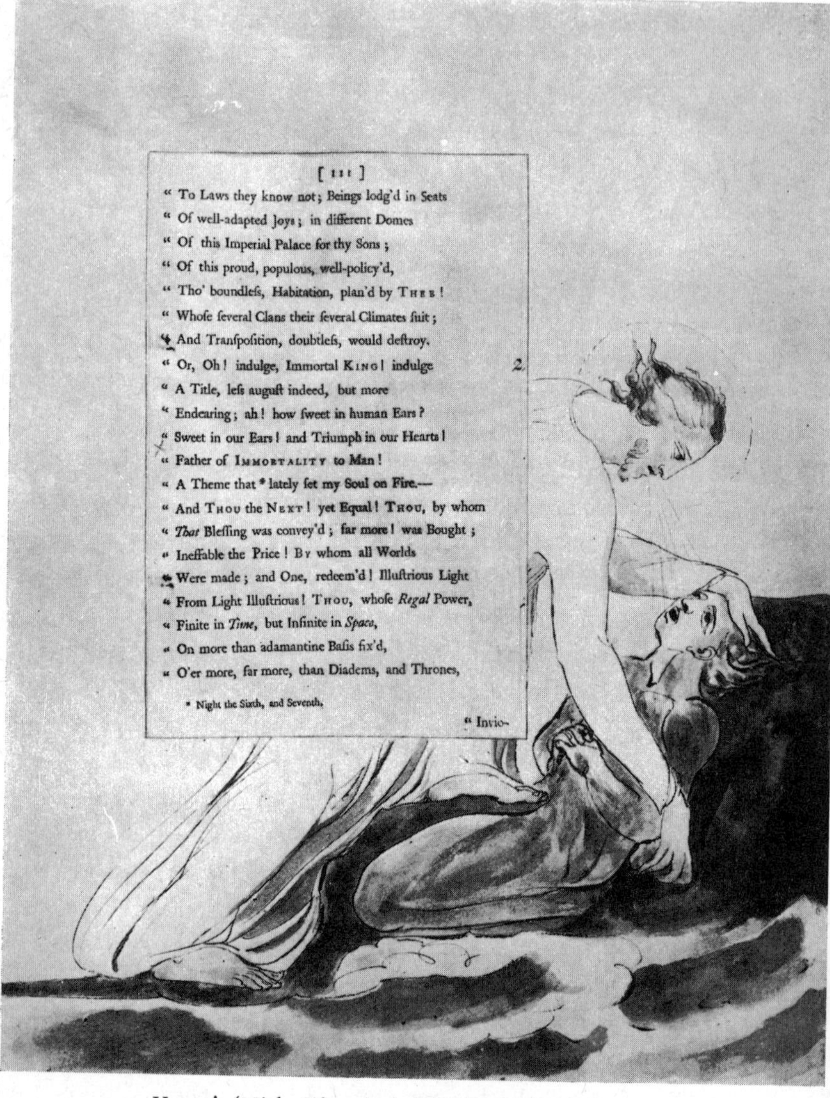
[111]

" To Laws they know not; Beings lodg'd in Seats
" Of well-adapted Joys; in different Domes
" Of this Imperial Palace for thy Sons;
" Of this proud, populous, well-policy'd,
" Tho' boundleſs, Habitation, plan'd by THEE!
" Whoſe ſeveral Clans their ſeveral Climates ſuit;
" And Tranſpoſition, doubtleſs, would deſtroy.
" Or, Oh! indulge, Immortal KING! indulge
" A Title, leſs auguſt indeed, but more
" Endearing; ah! how ſweet in human Ears?
" Sweet in our Ears! and Triumph in our Hearts!
" Father of IMMORTALITY to Man!
" A Theme that * lately ſet my Soul on Fire.—
" And THOU the NEXT! yet Equal! THOU, by whom
" *That* Bleſſing was convey'd; far more! was Bought;
" Ineffable the Price! BY whom all Worlds
" Were made; and One, redeem'd! Illuſtrious Light
" From Light Illuſtrious! THOU, whoſe *Regal* Power,
" Finite in *Time*, but Infinite in *Space*,
" On more than adamantine Baſis fix'd,
" O'er more, far more, than Diadems, and Thrones,

* Night the Sixth, and Seventh.

" Invio-

Young's 'Night Thoughts': Night IX, lines 2283–2303
Drawing by William Blake
(*Courtesy of The British Museum*)

tions, and dress or lack of dress. Life as a journey must have been much in Blake's mind at this time. His best-known drawing of a traveller, however, is earlier (1793). It is on plate 14 ('The Traveller hasteth in the Evening') of *The Gates of Paradise*. Not before 1824 did Blake do a set of illustrations for *The Pilgrim's Progress*, but in between, as I have pointed out elsewhere,[1] is the tiny figure of the pilgrim in the great *Milton* illustration of the huge trilithon and the pygmy horseman.

Blake had many experiences of fresh illumination. One of the most notable occurred when he was writing *Vala*. It made him change that poem (itself 'A Dream of Nine Nights' in titular imitation of Young) to *The Four Zoas*. It deeply concerned his understanding of Christ and Christianity. Can we from his depiction of Christ in these drawings get nearer his understanding of Christ before the illumination which occurred during the writing of *Vala*? One way of putting this question would be to ask whether the figure of Christ in these drawings is in a different class from the human figures of Time, Death, or Conscience or even from such non-human figures as the Serpent and the Tree.

Leaving aside such a picture as that of the Good Samaritan, where an equation with Christ may be suggested but need not be insisted upon, we find Christ, if I have counted right, in twenty-seven pictures. Of these, four are in Night IV, two in Night VI, one in Night VII, two in Night VIII, and eighteen in Night IX, which is much the longest Night. Five of the first seven are Resurrection pictures. These include the frontispiece to Night IV (called by Young 'The Christian Triumph') and a consecutive series of three, the last page of Night VI where Christ

[1] *William Blake*, 1951, p. 132.

rises naked, the remarkable end-piece to Night VI reproduced by Keynes, and the half-title to Night VII. Night VIII, p. 32, represents Christ seated under the tree of this life and receiving children, and p. 70 has the first temptation in the wilderness already mentioned (Satan the Dunce). The title of Night IX ('The Consolation') suggested to Blake the passage (Luke ii. 25) about Simeon 'waiting for the consolation of Israel'. The picture represents Anna in brown with outstretched left arm and Simeon in white holding the infant in his left hand. This is the only infant Jesus in the series.

The other seventeen in Night IX are very varied, but eight come almost in a block (pp. 109–11, 113–17). There are incidents—the woman with an issue of blood, Pilate asking 'What is Truth?', the Sower sowing, and a banquet difficult to identify with that at Cana or any other recorded. The dead Christ, Christ watching two disciples as fishers of men, Christ the Vine are also biblical. Christ as the Creator, Christ receiving souls or waiting above as an old man dies, Christ knocking at the door behind which the inmates wait ('True *Taste* of Life, and constant *Thought of Death*') are in another category. We begin to forget Young and to find only Blake in Christ depicted as 'Father of All', as 'Father fond' and as 'Father of Immortality to Man'. This last (p. 111) is Blake at his most Blakian. On a reddish-brown rock a clothed man leans back with his feet under him, his hands clasped and his face looking up rather like Adam in 'The Elohim creating Adam', to which, indeed, this seems a companion picture. Here Christ is striding, his right foot lower down the rock and his left on a level with the man's waist. He breathes (rayed lines) into the man's open mouth. Christ's left hand is on the top of the man's head, his right is gathering earth near the man's left elbow. This seems to depict the second of the two accounts in Genesis of the creation of man, 'and man became a living soul'.

With this picture the answer is clear. We have a person not a personification, or, if in a sense a personification, it is not of an experience such as Death, Time, or Conscience but of a self-subsisting reality, a personal Creator. Moreover, the Creator is Christ and beneficent, not the sinister Elohim of the great colour-print. Yet it seems also clear that Blake's Christianity at this time is, if one may so put it, of the highest Old Testament kind, in spite of the symbolical resurrections. The later crisis which played such havoc with *Vala*, gave him a Christianity of incarnation, sacrifice, and redemption—'the Lamb of God'.

The drawings are interesting in all sorts of other ways. For example, though Blake draws so many nudes and so many figures in what can only be called coloured tights, the drawings also abound in varieties of contemporary costume—hats, shoes, frocks, coats, breeches, frilled nightshirts—not to mention elaborate cushions, feminine hair fashions, and children's toys. One last matter may be selected for special mention, another personification or set of personifications. Many times we come on a female figure, by no means always the same, whom we instinctively want to call Vala, though Vala was a name as yet unknown to Blake's writings. Nature, Earth, Fortune, Venus may be her first name, but it is Vala (the Nature which can be a veil between man and his real life) that she is becoming, and most notably so in Night III, pp. 30 and 31. On p. 30 Blake illustrated the lines

> Is not the mighty *Mind* that Son of Heaven!
> By Tyrant *Life* dethron'd, imprison'd, pain'd?

On the left behind bars sits a man wearing a loose loin-cloth, with wrist and ankle chained, bowing his head on his hand. On the right, in a very strangely hunched but quite feasible attitude, sits a crowned naked woman with very long yellow hair. She is 'Life', that is to say the life of the senses only, of the purely 'material', and she keeps Man in a prison. In *Vala* she will be Vala and feed the fires of the 'furnaces of affliction' into which Luvah has been cast. It does not seem an extravagant guess that Blake's conception of Vala came to him while he was engaged on the *Night Thoughts*. Immediately after that engagement he started on the poem *Vala*, which in the end was disrupted by further illumination, was partly erased, partly rewritten, left chaotic. Yet this, like other guesses at elucidation, needs the help of many minds working for years on material readily at hand. Where would one be with Milton if a large section of his work were available only in a single copy in a public library? How can the large company of students of Blake function adequately when 457 drawings,[1] most of his work for a year and a half of the prime of his life, have never been reproduced?

[1] The number is now reduced to 453, as four of the drawings are reproduced for the first time in this book, two (The Temptation and The Creation) described in the article and two (The Miners and The Telescope) not.

IX

Blake's 'Ancient of Days' and Motte's Frontispiece to Newton's Principia

by

Martin K. Nurmi
Kent State University, Kent, Ohio (*U.S.A.*)

IX

Blake's 'Ancient of Days' and Motte's Frontispiece to Newton's Principia

THE COMPLEX OF elements contributing to Blake's 'The Ancient of Days' (*fig. 1*, the frontispiece to *Europe*) has been ably treated by Sir Anthony Blunt,[1] who has shown that, though we need not question Blake's own report of having seen his picture in a vision hovering over a staircase, this vision was considerably influenced by the traditional iconography of the compass. Calling attention to the appearance of a compass in Blake's colour print of Newton, Mr. Blunt has also shown that this traditional iconography was transformed in the frontispiece by Blake's anti-Newtonian philosophy, so that the figure shown drawing with a compass in the frontispiece is not the Creator, inscribing His lines of order upon chaos, but Blake's fallen demiurge, Urizen, constructing with the science of 'line & plummet' and 'golden compasses' [2] the Enlightenment's world of abstract categories, which Blake viewed as repressing man's divine nature.

We may get a hint as to a further detail in the evolution of Blake's frontispiece if we compare it with a picture of Newton and a compass, drawn by another artist with an intention quite different from Blake's. This comparison may even enable us to see why, after Blake had used the compass with its traditional

[1] Anthony Blunt, 'Blake's "Ancient of Days"', *Journal of the Warburg (and Courtauld) Institute(s)*, II, July, 1938, pp. 53–63.

[2] Blake, *The First Book of Urizen*, *Blake's Poetry and Prose*, ed. Geoffrey Keynes, London, 1948, p. 231.

meaning in his picture of 'Christ in the Carpenter's Shop,' [1] he should have made of it both in his picture of Newton and in his frontispiece to *Europe* a symbol of the anti-Christian modes of thought epitomized for him in the science of Newton. The other picture (*fig.* 2) is the frontispiece drawn and engraved by A. Motte for the first English translation of Newton's *Principia* (*The Mathematical Principles of Natural Philosophy*, trans. Andrew Motte (possibly the artist), London, 1729, 2 vols.).

We cannot be certain that Blake ever read the *Principia*, for he never expressly mentioned having done so. But if he did, it was probably in Motte's edition, since this was not only the standard English translation of the *Principia* of the eighteenth century, it was the only complete one.[2] In view of Blake's vigorous opposition to Newton, however, it would be surprising indeed if he had not familiarized himself with his 'spiritual enemy' at first hand, as he had familiarized himself with the major works of Bacon and Locke, the other members of the triumvirate which he believed to control the thought of his age. Newton's mathematical works, including the *Principia*, were, moreover, brought very much to the attention of the eighteenth century in a way that would give even a lay critic the confidence to examine them for himself. Even the fundamental question was debated whether natural philosophy could be reduced to mathematical principles.[3] And, by 1794, when Blake wrote and designed *Europe*, a continuous controversy had raged for sixty years over Newton's concept of 'limits', a concept basic to

[1] See Blunt, *op. cit.*, p. 60.

[2] One volume of a projected English translation by Robert Thorpe was issued in 1777, but the project was discontinued.

[3] See, for instance, Bishop George Horne's *A Fair, Candid, and Impartial State of the Case between Sir Isaac Newton and Mr. Hutchinson*, Oxford, 1753.

'The Ancient of Days' (Frontispiece to *Europe*)
Engraving by William Blake
(*Courtesy of The British Museum*)

Frontispiece to Newton's *Principia* translated by A. Motte, London, 1729
Engraving of design by A. Motte
(*Courtesy of the Columbia University Libraries*)

the calculus and first introduced in the *Principia.* After Berkeley's penetrating criticism of Newton's formulation of the idea (*The Analyst*, 1734), Newton's work was attacked and defended not only in pamphlets addressed to the learned, but also in such popular publications as *The Monthly Review, The Republick of Letters,* and even *The Ladies' Diary: or the Woman's Almanack.*[1]

Blake was well enough acquainted with the subject of this controversy to use Newton's doctrine of fluxions (the calculus) accurately and with admirable satiric effect to characterize the vagueness, as he saw it, of art and thought in the eighteenth century. In a letter written near the end of his life he remarks, 'I know too well that the great majority of Englishmen are fond of the indefinite, which they measure by Newton's doctrine of the fluxions of an atom, a thing which does not exist'.[2] Newton's 'fluxions', quantities which are by definition too small to have numerical value, would indeed be the appropriate measure of the 'indefinite' in an era of atomic materialism. And, though fluxions have nothing to do with atoms, Blake does not betray ignorance in the phrase 'fluxions of an atom'; he simply compounds his charge by reductively making the Newtonian measure of the indefinite an infinitesimal portion of a further infinitesimal, which, in turn, no one can demonstrate to exist.

This comment is the statement of 'an old man, feeble and tottering', as Blake described himself, summarizing the struggles of a lifetime. Probably he had known Newton's

[1] The history of this controversy is treated by Florian Cajori in *A History of the Conceptions of Limits and Fluxions in Great Britain from Newton to Woodhouse*, Chicago and London, 1919.

[2] Letter to Cumberland, 12 April 1827, Blake, *op. cit.*, pp. 926–927.

fluxions and limits for a long time. How long we cannot tell. But in his first attempt at 'illuminated printing', in 1788, he had probably in mind Newton's mathematical philosophy as that is set forth in the *Principia*, when he seized upon the word 'ratio' and made of it a sort of portmanteau epithet to sum up the thought of his time. 'Ratio', as Blake uses it, means not only *ratio* (reason) but mathematical proportion. The mathematical meaning is certainly paramount when he writes, in the tractate *There is No Natural Religion*, 'He who sees the Infinite in all things, sees God. He who sees the Ratio only, sees himself only'.[1] In the *Principia* Blake would have found 'ratio' used more often than almost any other word, especially in the early sections, where Newton sets forth his concept of limits.

More particular evidence for Blake's having seen the *Principia* and Motte's frontispiece, however, is to be found in the parallels between the two frontispieces themselves. While there is no similarity between the two main figures, aside from the fact that one foot of each is slightly extended, there are several significant parallels between the pictures as a whole: the compasses, the lighted spaces in the clouds,[2] the rays of light radiating from spheres (from the sun in Motte's picture and from, or possibly behind, Urizen's sphere in Blake's). There is even a general similarity in the compositional motif of the circle lying above the apex of an angle used by both men. (This motif is formed by the sun and the radii of the astronomical diagrams in Motte's picture, and by Urizen's sphere and the compass in Blake's.) And there are also two levels in both pictures, shown by Motte, implied by Blake: Urizen

[1] Blake, *op. cit.*, p. 148.

[2] A. G. B. Russell regards the clouds as smoke (*The Engravings of William Blake*, London, 1912, p. 70).

could, indeed, be viewed as being in the process of drawing the astronomical diagrams which appear in the lower part of Motte's picture.

It is true, of course, that Blake did not need Motte to help him conceive of his design. And a sufficient source for the symbolism, one with which Blake was thoroughly familiar, is to be found in the account of creation in Proverbs viii. 27, where the Almighty 'set a compass upon the face of the depths', an account which also appears in *Paradise Lost* vii. 225–231.[1] But at the same time, in considering works in which Blake criticized his age as sharply as he does in the frontispiece to *Europe*, it is often valuable, as Mr. David V. Erdman has demonstrated,[2] to look for concrete contemporary correspondences to his symbols, for doing so frequently yields results that not only shed light on Blake's methods, but give force and point to symbols that remain otherwise rather general or even obscure. The fact that compasses are associated with both the Almighty in Proverbs (though the primary meaning of the word there is circle) and with Newton, the astronomer, makes Blake's visual symbol of the frontispiece quite easily comprehensible as a general critical commentary on the religion and thought of his age. But this symbol becomes a more compelling one, and the ironic identification of Newton with the Almighty becomes a less harsh and arbitrary treatment of the scientist, whom Blake regarded as less a *cause* than a victim of anti-visionary attitudes, if we discover that Blake was responding critically to something in which such an identification, and not an ironic one, had actually been made. He would have seen it in

[1] In Daniel vii. 9–10 the Ancient of Days is described as wearing a garment 'white as snow' and as having hair 'like the pure wool'.

[2] *Blake: Prophet Against Empire*, Princeton, 1954.

Motte's picture. Indeed, if we accept the hypothesis that Blake was responding to Motte's picture, viewed in this light, we can also account for several features of his design as showing him practicing his favourite method of attacking spiritual enemies, that of turning their own ideas against them, hoisting them with their own petards.

It is doubtful whether Motte really intended to compare Newton with God. More likely he intended nothing more than a conventionally hyperbolic canonization or a vague apotheosis of Newton.[1] He places him in a circle of celestial light, with his body in an attitude reminiscent of saintly inspiration and annunciation, receiving divine inspiration, or gratitude, from naked Truth, who holds the compass with which Newton's inspired work was done. Motte's picture, reflecting the secularization of themes from religious painting that had occurred since the Renaissance, is probably meant to attribute no more of divinity to Newton than to suggest that he was divinely appointed to reveal the wonders of creation to man. Thomson, in his poetic encomium 'To the Memory of Sir Isaac Newton' written two years earlier, had paid perhaps a more exaggerated compliment by implying that heaven itself would have few new wonders to show the spirit of the illustrious scientist.

Blake, however, viewing Motte's picture from the uncompromising perspective of prophecy, would have responded neither conventionally nor charitably. Even if Motte had intended no Biblical allusion, Blake would have seen one, and his response might well have been, 'True! Here is plain confession that man's rational spectre now is god'. In an age in which, as

[1] Cf. Blake's calling Newton 'St. Isaac' in *The Everlasting Gospel*, Blake, *op. cit.*, p. 137.

Blake saw it, everything but reason and the evidence of the five senses was rejected as nothing but 'delusion and fancy', Motte's picture would afford added and literal confirmation of the truth that the reasoning power, 'the terrible destroyer, & not the Saviour', was worshipped.[1]

In his own picture Blake seems to bring out what would have struck him as the real meaning of Motte's; he reveals the truth contained, unintentionally, in the hyperbole, showing by what appear to be transformations of Motte's symbolism the true nature of the god implied by Motte's conception. Whereas Motte had portrayed Newton as a rather passive old man, Blake portrays Urizen as a very active old god, as an oppressor and a destroyer, in fact, stabbing down into the abyss with a compass that has become an instrument of impalement. Whereas Motte had placed Newton in a spacious heaven, Blake shows the true scope of 'natural religion' by squeezing Urizen into a tightly bounding sphere. Whereas Motte had shown Newton basking in celestial light and receiving inspiration, Blake turns Urizen away from the light and makes him peer down into the darkness. Finally, whereas Motte had indicated that Newton inhabited both heaven and earth, Blake places Urizen down where he belongs, in the sphere of the material sun, in the centre of the 'Substantial Astronomical Telescopic Heavens' [2] which Newton's astronomy had charted, and suggests that Urizen's creation lies below, in the abyss. In short, Blake shows that the creation of a Newtonian god is an 'unprolific, / Self-clos'd, all repelling' and 'abominable void', a 'soul-shuddering vacuum', as he described it in the same year in *The Book of Urizen*.[3]

Such a reverse transformation of Motte's symbolism is

[1] Blake, *op. cit.*, p. 260. [2] *Ibid.*, p. 827. [3] *Ibid.*, p. 220.

perfectly characteristic of Blake. He does something similar in *The Marriage of Heaven and Hell*, for instance, where he uses Swedenborg's ideas, symbolism, and 'memorable relations' of life among the angels to satirize him. Indeed, the method of critical irony is so characteristic of Blake that it penetrates the very structure of his central myth of the fall. In *The Book of Urizen*, where he first elaborates his myth, he shows that a world based on the Newtonian premiss of substantiality will inevitably be just the opposite of what the Newtonians desire. Urizen, unable to endure the creative mental life of Eden, sets out to create a material world that is 'solid without fluctuation', but succeeds only in bringing about a fallen world which not only fluctuates, but whose main feature is fluctuation: it is constantly torn by a regular and destructively cyclical alternation between oppression and revolt.[1] Perhaps more than is generally recognized, even some of Blake's positive concepts, such as his doctrine of imaginative perception and certain aspects of his cosmology, owe their form to their being critical transformations of the ideas of those he opposes. Locke's having based his epistemology on physical sense perception is an important reason why Blake should have based his own on the 'spiritual perception' of the imagination; imagination need not be thought of as a kind of perception at all. And Newton's concept of 'nascent and evanascent limits' may have been the original which Blake transformed into the 'limits' of opacity and translucence, contraction and expansion, which form such an important feature of the structure of his visionary cosmos.

In at least one other picture, moreover, Blake took over a portion of another man's design and transformed it in such a

[1] See Northrop Frye, *Fearful Symmetry: A Study of William Blake*, Princeton, 1947, p. 221.

way that he makes a pictorial rejoinder, as he seems to do in the frontispiece to *Europe*. In 'I want! I want!' (plate nine of *The Gates of Paradise*), as Mr. Erdman has discovered, Blake originally responded to a political cartoon by James Gillray. Gillray's satiric print, *The Slough of Despond: Vide the Patriot's Progress*, shows the ladder leading from 'Libertas' to the patriot's 'Promised Land' on the moon as being too short. 'Blake's response to this piece of cynicism,' remarks Mr. Erdman, 'was to draw an extension to the ladder long enough to reach the moon and a youthful pilgrim energetic enough to climb it.'[1]

I do not wish to suggest that Blake's frontispiece to *Europe* is merely, or even primarily, a critical response to Motte; Blake is not to be thus explained by his sources. As Mr. Erdman points out, 'I want! I want!' though political in origin, becomes something much more inclusive as one of the series of emblematic plates and verses which answers the question, 'What is man?' In the frontispiece to *Europe* Blake makes a prophetic comment, not on Motte, but on a great and prevalent error, of which Motte, Thomson—and even Newton himself—are only symptoms; and he does so in the hope that this error will not always prevail, that man's now fallen rational nature will ultimately be transformed and restored to its proper sphere in the wholeness of 'humanity'. Moreover, Blake's conception of the picture undergoes subtle modulations as he colours it. Nevertheless, the meaning of the picture as a whole becomes clearer when we view it, if only hypothetically, as having been prompted by Motte, for Motte's frontispiece to the *Principia* perfectly epitomizes the attitudes and ideas Blake was attacking. If Motte was not a 'source' (a negative one), he ought to have been.

[1] See Erdman, *op. cit.*, pp. 186–187.

That Blake may in some measure actually have been responding to Motte, however, is suggested not only by the points of contact which we have noted between the symbolism and designs of the two pictures, but by echoes of Motte in the text of *Europe*. Newton, curiously prominent in *Europe* in view of the fact that it is a political prophecy, appears at the climax of the work, apotheosized very much as Motte had shown him, as a 'mighty Spirit'. And a little earlier, man's repression by natural religion is described in terms quite reminiscent of Motte's Newtonian astronomical diagram: the eternal forests were divided 'into earths rolling in circles of space', the 'image of the infinite/(was) Shut up in finite revolutions', and heaven had become 'a mighty circle turning'.[1]

[1] Blake, *op. cit.*, pp. 217, 216.